S. HRG. 114–519

UNITED NATIONS PEACEKEEPING AND OPPORTUNITIES FOR REFORM

HEARING

BEFORE THE

COMMITTEE ON FOREIGN RELATIONS UNITED STATES SENATE

ONE HUNDRED FOURTEENTH CONGRESS

FIRST SESSION

DECEMBER 9, 2015

Printed for the use of the Committee on Foreign Relations

Available via the World Wide Web: http://www.gpo.gov/fdsys/

U.S. GOVERNMENT PUBLISHING OFFICE

23–034 PDF   WASHINGTON : 2016

For sale by the Superintendent of Documents, U.S. Government Publishing Office
Internet: bookstore.gpo.gov Phone: toll free (866) 512–1800; DC area (202) 512–1800
Fax: (202) 512–2104 Mail: Stop IDCC, Washington, DC 20402–0001

(II)

CONTENTS

ADDITIONAL MATERIAL SUBMITTED FOR THE RECORD

UNITED NATIONS PEACEKEEPING AND OPPORTUNITIES FOR REFORM

Wednesday, December 9, 2015

U.S. SENATE,
COMMITTEE ON FOREIGN RELATIONS,
Washington, DC.

The committee met, pursuant to notice, at 9:32 a.m., in Room SD–419, Dirksen Senate Office Building, Hon. Bob Corker, chairman of the committee, presiding.

Present: Senators Corker [presiding], Johnson, Flake, Gardner, Perdue, Isakson, Barrasso, Cardin, Menendez, Shaheen, Coons, Udall, Murphy, Kaine, and Markey.

OPENING STATEMENT OF HON. BOB CORKER, U.S. SENATOR FROM TENNESSEE

The CHAIRMAN. The Senate Foreign Relations Committee will come to order.

I want to thank our witness. I know she has significant responsibilities right now at the U.N. Security Council. Ben and I had a chance this week to meet with her and all the members. Quite educational, I hope on both sides. But we certainly appreciate you being here, and I will introduce you in just a moment.

Today's hearing will review the United Nations peacekeeping operations and explore opportunities for reform to make U.N. peacekeeping work better in U.S. national interests.

As a permanent member of the Security Council and the largest contributor by far to the U.N. peacekeeping budget, the U.S. has a particular interest in how U.N. peacekeeping mandates are set and operations are carried out. The United States cannot be everywhere all the time. There is an important role for U.N. peacekeeping in supporting U.S. interests for security and stability around the world.

Today's U.N. peacekeeping is evolving in many ways. Traditionally, missions have focused primarily on negotiating peace agreements, inserting blue helmets to separate conflicting parties to implement these agreements, and generally monitoring and keeping the peace.

U.N. peacekeepers now are being asked to take on new and difficult responsibilities, such as civilian protection, disarming active combatants, or developing the capacity to engage on the antiterrorism front. These new missions and mandates raise many questions, which we certainly will be exploring today.

What are the risks when U.N. peacekeepers actively engage combatants in a warzone? Do U.N. peacekeepers forgo their neutrality in these instances? And if so, what are the implications for our interests?

If U.N. peacekeepers are asked to provide logistics support in humanitarian crises such as the Ebola fight in West Africa, what challenges does that raise?

I am particularly concerned with recent disturbing reports of sexual exploitation and abuse by certain U.N. peacekeeping troops. The current U.N. policy is zero tolerance, but such abuses continue with disturbing regularity.

So it is our hope to find some common sense ways to address these issues and explore these and other topics, such as the U.S. peacekeeping assessment.

We again want to thank our distinguished witness for being here, and I will turn it over to our ranking member for his comments.

STATEMENT OF HON. BENJAMIN L. CARDIN, U.S. SENATOR FROM MARYLAND

Senator CARDIN. Well, thank you, Chairman Corker. I very much appreciate you convening this hearing on an important topic, and I want to thank all of our distinguished panelists today, extraordinary individuals who have given so much to our country. We thank you all for your participation and your continued service to our country, particularly Ambassador Powers.

It is good to see you here.

I have long believed the United Nations at its best can be a powerful partner of the United States, advancing global peace and security for far less cost and more effectively than if we act alone. When you add the U.N. presence, it is a global presence, and that is far preferable than having a U.S. or sole, one-country presence.

The U.N. does many things right. They assist more than 60 million refugees and displaced people fleeing conflict, famine, and persecution with lifesaving assistance. It provides food to 90 million people in 80 countries. It vaccinates 58 percent of the world's children, saving no less than 3 million lives.

Recently, it launched the sustainable development goals, which it fully embraced. It could have a powerful impact globally on reducing corruption and poor governance.

In short, the U.N. is capable of and has already done a great deal of good in the world. But I believe that the U.N. could be stronger and much more effective, if there were greater transparency and accountability across the entire organization.

The U.N.'s continuing anti-Israel bias is deeply unhelpful to our shared interests in a peaceful, stable Middle East.

In the case of Syria, the Assad regime continues its indiscriminate barrel-bombing and slaughter of civilians. And those responsible for war crimes have yet to be held accountable.

But let us be clear. The United States could not ensure international security alone nor should it have to. The United Nations and specifically the U.N. peacekeeping remains one of the best burden-sharing tools we have to help end war, protect civilian population, and secure territory.

By drawing upon the financial and human capacities of all U.N. member states, the U.N. peacekeeping helps the United States share the responsibility of promoting global stability and reduces the need for unilateral intervention.

United Nations peacekeeping has managed to protect hundreds of thousands of innocent civilians. With more than 120,000 military and police personnel currently serving as part of 16 missions on four continents, U.N. peacekeepers now represent the largest deployed military force in the world.

There are more U.N. peacekeeping missions today because peacekeepers are being asked to do more in increasingly dangerous, remote, and deadly operational environments. We need to recognize this and make sure that the United Nations and the troop-contributing countries are given peacekeepers who are placed in harm's way the protective equipment, training, and support that they deserve.

Peacekeepers themselves are often seen as legitimate targets for attack by extremist groups and others. We saw that recently in the horrific attacks in Mali, where terrorists linked to al Qaeda killed 20 people, including an American from Maryland. The U.N. peacekeeping mission in Mali has suffered 42 fatalities at the hands of the militants since January 2013.

We know that the U.N. peacekeeping is a cost-effective tool when compared to other military options. The U.N. annual peacekeeping budget only makes up about 0.5 percent of the world's total military expenditures.

I think this is a particularly important moment, considering that we are debating the omnibus and dealing with the fiscal issues of our country and trying balance our budgets, so let me bring it closer to home. The U.N. mission, the cost per peacekeeper per year, is about $16,000. In 2014, each U.S. soldier in Afghanistan cost $2.1 million. Moreover, according to the study by the GAO, U.N. peacekeeping operations are eight times less expensive than funding a comparable U.S. force.

This is not to say the U.S. share of peacekeeping dues should continue unchanged. I think the chairman has raised a good point about reform in the United Nations in the way they do their budget. The scaled assessment should be reworked, and I am confident that Ambassador Power and the U.N. team are focused on that goal as well.

Maintaining the legitimacy of the U.N. peacekeeping is essential. Nothing will erode it faster than the horrific reports that we received on sexual abuse by peacekeepers in certain missions.

I have long been concerned about these disturbing reports of sexual exploitation and abuse. As the largest contributor to the United Nations and as the permanent member on the U.N. Security Council, the United States has a responsibility to ensure that the United Nations uphold the highest standards of professionalism in peacekeeping operations. The failure by the United Nations to hold individual peacekeepers, their commanders, and troop-contributing countries accountable for verifiable allegations of abuse is unacceptable.

U.N. Secretary General Ban Ki-Moon recently announced a series of proposals to combat sexual exploitation and abuse in peacekeeping at a meeting of the representatives from over 100 troop-contributing countries. That is only a start. More must be done by both the United Nations and the member states. And I look forward to hearing about how the United States can continue to push for these effective reforms.

I look forward to hearing from our witnesses and having a robust discussion.

The CHAIRMAN. Thank you, Senator Cardin.

We have two distinguished panels today, and we want to thank all who are here to share their wisdom.

Our first witness is the Permanent Representative to the U.S. Mission to the United Nations, Samantha Power. We thank you for being here today with a very tight schedule.

We also thank you for bringing Haley back, who served so well with Senator Coons here and was one of the bright people we had here on the committee amongst many.

But we thank you both for being here. If you could keep your comments to about 5 minutes or so, we would appreciate it, and then we look forward to Q&A. Thank you.

STATEMENT OF HON. SAMANTHA POWER, UNITED STATES PERMANENT REPRESENTATIVE TO THE UNITED NATIONS, UNITED STATES MISSION TO THE UNITED NATIONS, NEW YORK, NEW YORK

Ambassador POWER. Thank you so much, Mr. Chairman, Ranking Member Cardin, for convening this hearing. And thank you all, distinguished members of the committee, for making time to be here to discuss peacekeeping.

This committee is acutely aware of the extent to which conflicts on the other side of the globe can come back and threaten American security. We have seen time and again how conflicts can displace millions of people, upend markets, and destabilize entire regions.

All too recently and all too frequently, we have seen how such instability can attract and enable violent extremist groups, who exploit the vacuum of authority to terrorize civilians; recruit new members; and plan, launch, or inspire attacks.

U.N. peacekeepers play a vital role in the international community's efforts to address war, violence, and instability. As President Obama said in September, "We know that peace operations are not the solution to every problem, but they do remain one of the world's most important tools to address armed conflict."

Peacekeepers can help resolve conflict, shore up stability, deny safe harbor to extremists, and protect civilians from atrocities, all of which serve core American interests and reflect deep American values, while ensuring greater burden-sharing by the international community.

This administration has consequently been working aggressively to ensure that U.N. peacekeeping operations are better able to meet the demands of international peace and security, which, as has been noted by both the chairman and the ranking member, those requirements have changed considerably over just the last 20 years.

Peacekeepers today are undertaking more missions. The number of uniformed personnel has risen from fewer than 20,000 15 years ago to over 100,000 today.

They are assuming greater risk. Two-thirds of peacekeepers are operating in active conflicts, the highest percentage in history.

And they are assigned broad and increasingly complex responsibilities, ranging from disarming armed groups to facilitating the safe delivery of humanitarian aid to protecting civilians from those who wish them harm.

Today, 98 percent of uniformed personnel in U.N. missions around the world are under orders to protect civilians as part of their mandate. This is not your mother's peacekeeping, your father's peacekeeping, your grandfather's peacekeeping. It has evolved significantly.

While peacekeeping has never been more important to American interests, it has also never been more demanding. And that is why, in September, President Obama issued the first presidential memorandum on multilateral peace operations in more than 20 years, directing a wide range of actions to strengthen and modernize U.N. operations, including by building partner capacity, providing U.S. support, and leading reform of U.N. peacekeeping.

I just want to briefly, Mr. Chairman, touch on a few key lines of effort that we have pursued. These are described in greater detail in my written submission.

First, we are working to ensure that countries with the will to perform 21st century peacekeeping, that they have the capacity to do so. One way we are doing this is through the African Peacekeeping Rapid Response Partnership, or APRRP, which President Obama announced in August 2014.

Through APRRP, the United States is investing in the capacity of six African countries that have proven themselves leaders in peacekeeping. In exchange, these countries have committed to maintain the forces and equipment necessary to deploy rapidly.

This initiative builds upon the Global Peace Operations Initiative launched under President George W. Bush, which is our primary tool for building partner-nation peacekeeping capacity, and it will help ensure that more soldiers deployed for peacekeeping missions will be fully prepared.

I hope that the Senate and House will fully fund this important initiative in future years.

Second, we are expanding the pool of troop- and police-contributing countries, and bringing advanced militaries back into peacekeeping. In September, President Obama convened a historic high-level summit, the first of its kind, at the U.N. to rally new commitments to peacekeeping, marking the culmination of a yearlong effort initiated by Vice President Biden at the previous U.N. General Assembly. Forty-nine countries participated and pledged nearly 50,000 additional troops and police.

Not only that, more of these troops will now come from advanced militaries, who bring with them equipment and expertise that is critically needed on the ground. We saw this in Mali in January this year, when Dutch attack helicopters helped Bangladeshi infantry repel rebels who had opened fire on their camp, where civilians were taking refuge.

The United States is making contributions in this respect as well as one part of our unrivaled contribution to global peace and security, looking specifically for ways to leverage our military's unique capabilities to support peacekeeping operations, including by enabling faster deployment by others.

Third, we are working to ensure a higher standard of performance and conduct once peacekeeping contingents are deployed, specifically in two critical areas: the complete fulfillment of their mandates and the combating of sexual exploitation and abuse.

The additional troops generated by the President's September summit will prove invaluable to both goals, by allowing the U.N. to be more selective as to which troops it deploys, and now giving it the leverage to repatriate poorly performing troops and police when necessary, and especially, of course, in instances where there are credible allegations of sexual abuse.

With respect to mandate, when peacekeepers deploy in volatile situations, they have to be prepared to use force to defend themselves, to protect civilians, and to otherwise carry out their mandated tasks.

Too often in the past, peacekeepers have shied away, even when atrocities are being perpetrated. A report by the U.N.'s internal oversight office in March last year found that in 507 attacks against civilians from 2010 to 2013, peacekeepers virtually never used force to protect those coming under attack. Thousands of civilians likely lost their lives as a result. This cannot continue, and a growing number of leading troop contributors agree. The 50,000 additional troops and police should enable more capable, more willing troops and police to staff these missions.

The same is true on sexual exploitation and violence. And let me just state the obvious here. We share the outrage of everyone on this committee, all the American people who are focused on this issue. Peacekeepers must not abuse civilians. Sexual abuse and exploitation have no place, it goes without saying, again, in any society. It is especially abhorrent when committed by those who take advantage of the trust that communities are placing in the United Nations, and those responsible must be held accountable.

Addressing this scourge will require continuing the important efforts begun by Secretary General Ban Ki-moon to strengthen the implementation of a zero-tolerance policy, including bolstering reporting and accountability measures, and pledging to set up an immediate response team to investigate certain cases. It will also require more vigilance and follow-through from troop-contributing countries.

There must also be far more transparency in these investigations, to track cases and ensure that justice is served.

The U.N. should be able to take advantage now of its newly expanded pool of soldiers and police by suspending from peacekeeping any country that does not take seriously the responsibility to investigate and, if necessary, prosecute credible allegations.

The fourth and final priority, Mr. Chairman, is to press for bold institutional reforms within the U.N. itself. We have seen the U.N. secretariat make profound changes to peacekeeping, from improved logistics and sustainment to a more comprehensive approach to crisis situations that integrates military, police, and civilian tools. But much, much more needs to be done, and we have spearheaded efforts to enact further reforms, including longer troop rotations to preserve institutional memory, penalties for troops who show up without the necessary equipment to perform their duties.

And we will continue to work aggressively to cut costs. The U.N. has already, thanks to U.S. leadership, cut the per-peacekeeper costs by roughly 17 percent since 2008. We are also working to advance the reforms proposed by the Secretary General's High-Level Independent Panel on U.N. Peace Operations, which are intended to address inadequate planning, slow troop deployment, uneven mission leadership, breakdowns in command-and-control, and a current set of rules around human resources and procurement designed for the conference rooms of New York and not the streets of Bangui.

Let me conclude. In all of the areas I have just described, we have seen improvements, and the United States has played an instrumental role in making them possible. But there is much more to be done.

We are not satisfied with peacekeepers fulfilling only parts, but not all, of their mandates; with peacekeepers standing up to protect civilians in some, but not all, situations; or with soldiers being held accountable for crimes or misconduct some, but not all, of the time.

The role played by peacekeepers today is too important. For the sake of our own interests and security, as well as the millions of innocent people around the world whose lives may depend on peacekeepers, we will continue working to strengthen peacekeeping so that it is tailored for the 21st century threats peacekeepers face.

We appreciate your interest and support and continued dialogue on these matters. Thank you.

[The prepared statement of Ambassador Power follows:]

PREPARED STATEMENT OF HON. SAMANTHA POWER

Chairman Corker, Ranking Member Cardin, distinguished members of the Committee, thank you for the invitation to testify today. I am grateful for this panel's enduring commitment to American leadership at the United Nations and in the world. And I appreciate the rigor that your members bring to ensuring the oversight and effective use of our contributions to the United Nations—a goal we share. I am grateful for the opportunity to discuss why the United States has such a strong interest in the success of U.N. peacekeeping and the Administration's strategy for strengthening this critical national security instrument.

First, I will discuss the growth and evolution of U.N. peacekeeping over the last decade, including the changing nature of these missions. Second, I will summarize the Administration's vision for strengthening U.N. peace operations, including by ensuring that troops and police in U.N. operations perform professionally and effectively. Third, I will describe U.S. support for peacekeeping, including the pledges made in the recently-issued Presidential Memorandum on U.S. Support to U.N. Peace Operations and at the recent Leaders' Summit on Peacekeeping at the U.N.

Evolution of U.N. Peacekeeping

The United States has a vital interest in strengthening peacekeeping to respond to demands that peacekeepers are currently struggling to meet. We do not want to live in a world where more than 9,000 children worldwide have been recruited in less than a year to become child soldiers, as happened in South Sudan. We do not want to live in a world where religious or ethnic communities who lived together for decades in harmony, such as the Muslims and Christians in the Central African Republic, are induced to hate and fear one another. We do not want to live in a world where violent extremists exploit weak governments and commit acts of terrorism, as we have seen in Somalia and recently witnessed in Mali. Nor, of course, do America's foreign policy leaders, including the distinguished members of this Committee.

Recognizing that our security and our values prevent us from ignoring these conflicts, the question remains: what can America do to stop them? Even if the United

States has an interest in seeing conflict abate or civilians protected, that does not mean that U.S. forces should be doing all of the abating or the protecting. As President Obama said at West Point last year, "America must always lead on the world stage," but "we should not go it alone." It should go without saying that we cannot and we should not send the U.S. military into all of the places conflict is burning, civilians are hurting, or extremists are lurking. Just because we have far and away the most capable military in the world does not mean we should assume risks and burdens that should be shared by the international community.

This is where peacekeeping comes in. As President Obama affirmed at the U.N. Leaders' Summit on Peacekeeping on September 28, 2015, "We know that peace operations are not the solution to every problem, but they do remain one of the world's most important tools to address armed conflict." When boots on the ground are needed to defuse conflict in Congo or Mali, peacekeeping is often the best instrument we have. Peacekeeping operations ensure that other countries help shoulder the burden, both by contributing uniformed personnel and by sharing the financial costs of the operations. Provided that peacekeepers actually deliver on their mandate, multilateral peacekeeping also brings a greater degree of legitimacy in the eyes of the local population and the world. Because missions are made up of troops from multiple countries, with strong representation from the global South, spoilers and militants have a harder time cynically branding them as having imperialist designs.

The U.N. has been there at critical junctures to consolidate peace and security and provide much needed stability after U.S. forces or our allies have been deployed for peace enforcement or stabilization operations, as in Haiti, Kosovo and Timor-Leste.

We have a compelling interest in curbing violent conflicts and preventing suffering—and we need peacekeeping to work. But precisely at this moment, when we recognize the crucial role peacekeeping can play in shoring up international security interests, our demands on peacekeeping are outstripping what it can deliver. Today, we are asking peacekeepers to do more, in more places, and in more complex conflicts than at any time in history.

The United States, during both Republican and Democratic administrations, has turned to peacekeeping operations to advance our national security interests. There are currently sixteen U.N. peacekeeping missions worldwide, made up of over 100,000 uniformed personnel, not to mention the 20,000 troops that the African Union currently deploys in Somalia. This is up from fewer than 20,000 fifteen years ago and 50,000 ten years ago.

To stress, this is by far the largest number of peacekeepers deployed in history. But the numbers only tell a small part of the story. Today, two-thirds of peacekeepers are operating in active conflicts, the highest percentage ever. Peacekeepers often deploy to areas where myriad rebel groups and militias have made clear their intention to keep fighting. And the warring parties in modern conflicts increasingly include violent extremist groups, who terrorize civilians and attack peacekeepers.

We are also asking peacekeepers to take on more responsibilities in support of sustainable political solutions. We ask U.N. peacekeeping missions to help with peace processes, assist with re-establishing state authority and stabilizing states amid deadly attacks by violent extremists, such as in Mali. We ask them to support the safe delivery of life-saving humanitarian assistance, such as escorting emergency shipments of food and medicine to civilians, as peacekeepers have done in South Sudan. We ask them to protect civilians from atrocities, as in the Central African Republic (CAR). We ask them to bolster security in countries emerging from brutal civil wars, such as in Liberia and Cote d'Ivoire, and to bolster regional stability from the Levant to the Great Lakes of Africa.

Precisely at this moment—when we are asking more of peacekeeping than ever before and as we recognize the crucial role it can play in protecting U.S. interests in just about every mission around the world—we see both the promise and the pitfalls of contemporary peacekeeping. We see life-saving impact when peacekeepers are willing and able to fulfill their mandates and the devastating consequences when they are not.

In the 21st century, the challenges to U.N. peacekeeping have changed, and so the international community's response must change with it. The United Nations is increasingly central to efforts to bring stability to the world's conflict zones, but too many U.N. peacekeeping operations are struggling to meet the demands placed upon them. Missions suffer from operational challenges, including long and overly complicated mandates, inadequate planning, obstacles to force generation, slow deployments, weak leadership, lack of critical enablers, competing chains of command, uneven commitments among troop—and police—contributing countries to mandate implementation, and political and administrative obstacles to operations created by the governments hosting peacekeepers. Additionally, each mission needs a strong political dialogue and agreement underpinning its efforts, a premise of their success.

U.S. Strategy for Strengthening Peacekeeping

On September 28, the day of the Leaders' Summit on Peacekeeping, President Obama issued a new policy Memorandum on U.S. Support to Peace Operations, the first presidential guidance to address U.S. support to peace operations in over twenty years. The policy reaffirms the strong support of the United States for U.N. peace operations and directs the interagency to take on a wide range of actions to strengthen and modernize U.N. operations for a new era. Our strategy prioritizes three lines of effort: building partner capacity and strengthening partner accountability; providing U.S. support; and leading reform of U.N. peacekeeping. I will now outline these efforts in detail.

First, we need to expand and deepen the pool of troop—and police—contributing countries, and bring advanced militaries back into peacekeeping. At the U.N. Leaders' Summit on Peacekeeping hosted by President Obama, the Secretary-General and eight other Member States, high-level leaders from 49 countries and three international organizations made pledges that far exceeded our expectations.

Twenty-one European countries made pledges, marking a welcome return of Europe to U.N. peacekeeping. Malaysia announced significant infantry, police, and engineering capabilities. Finland pledged multiple military units, including special forces. Chile—helicopters, hospitals, and engineering units. Colombia declared its intent to deploy multiple infantry battalions over the next few years. And China announced that it will establish a significant standby force that will be ready to deploy immediately in times of crises.

Leaders from every part of the world pledged approximately 12 field hospitals, 15 engineering companies, and 40 helicopters, as well as approximately 20 formed police units and over two-dozen infantry battalions. At the summit, and in the days that followed, countries committed to providing nearly 50,000 additional troops and police to U.N. peacekeeping. If countries deliver on these contributions—and we will join the U.N. in ensuring that they do—UN peacekeeping will be positioned to improve significantly its performance. The U.N. will have the capacity to fill long-standing gaps in operations—from attack helicopters to intelligence, surveillance, and reconnaissance units. If a new mission is created or an existing one significantly expanded, as sadly is sometimes the case, the U.N. will be able to put troops and police more quickly into the field.

Second, we need to ensure that countries with the will to perform 21st century peacekeeping have the capacity they need to do so. Because African leaders see first-hand the consequences of unchecked conflicts, several have been at the forefront of embracing a new approach to peacekeeping, one that seeks to more effectively execute the tasks assigned to peacekeepers and in particular the responsibility to protect civilians. The African Union has demonstrated a commitment to building rapid response capability on the continent, and the United States is leading a coalition of international partners in support of these efforts. Last year, President Obama announced a new initiative at the U.S.-Africa Leaders' Summit: the African Peacekeeping Rapid Response Partnership (APRRP). The United States is investing in the capacity of a core group of six countries—Ethiopia, Ghana, Rwanda, Senegal, Tanzania, and Uganda.

The idea is to deepen our investment in those militaries that have a track record of deploying troops to peacekeeping operations and that are committed to protecting civilians from violence. To give just one example, Rwanda's troops were among the first boots on the ground when conflicts erupted in the Central Africa Republic. Rwandans understand the importance of getting peacekeeping right, having experienced the catastrophic consequences of it going terribly wrong. And because Rwandans robustly carry out their mission mandates, the people in countries where they serve trust them; troops from other countries who serve alongside them see what robust peacekeeping looks like; and aggressors who would attack civilians fear them.

The United States remains the largest trainer and equipper of military and police contingents deploying to peacekeeping operations. We have trained hundreds of thousands of peacekeepers in the past decade through the Global Peace Operations Initiative (GPOI), launched under President Bush. While we must ensure the GPOI program remains robust and responsive, as it serves as our primary tool for building partner nations' peacekeeping capacities, APRRP is an important supplement. Our military experts will work alongside partners like Rwanda to strengthen their institutions and capabilities so they can rapidly deploy troops when crises emerge, and supply and sustain their forces in hostile environments. In exchange for this support, these countries have committed to maintain the forces and equipment necessary to undertake those rapid deployments. I strongly encourage the Senate and House to fully fund this important initiative in future years.

Third, we need to ensure that peacekeepers perform what is asked of them. Some troop-contributors disagree with the scope of responsibilities that the Security Council has assigned their troops. These countries sometimes cite the basic principles of U.N. peacekeeping, and hearken back to the earliest peacekeeping missions—in which blue helmets were deployed at the invitation of warring parties to observe a ceasefire along a demarcated line, such as one between Israel and Syria, or India and Pakistan. In that context, it was absolutely vital that peacekeepers had the states parties' consent, that they behaved impartially, and that they observed and reported infractions.

These missions are still critical, but for more than twenty years, peacekeeping has been evolving. The Security Council first tasked a peacekeeping mission with the responsibility to protect civilians in Sierra Leone in 1999—in the face of the brutal civil war in that country. While it is national governments' responsibility to take care of their own people, peacekeeping operations have a vital obligation to step in when they fail to do so. This duty is not theoretical. Today, 10 missions—constituting almost 98 percent of U.N. uniformed personnel across the world—are charged with protecting civilians. If peacekeeping is to be effective in the 21st century, we must close the gap between the mandates the international community asks peacekeepers to undertake, and the willingness and ability of peacekeepers to successfully execute them. If we do not, it not only puts the lives of civilians and peacekeepers at risk, but undermines the credibility and legitimacy of peacekeeping everywhere. This is one of the most important efforts underway today.

The good news is that there is a growing consensus around what modern peacekeeping looks like. In May, drawing on its direct knowledge of what it means when U.N. peacekeepers do not protect civilians, Rwanda channeled its lessons learned from the field into a set of best practices for the protection of civilians by peacekeeping missions. These "Kigali Principles" call, for example, for troop-contributing countries to ensure that the military commander of a peacekeeping contingent has prior authority to use force as needed. When a commander has to radio back to capital to seek permission, it may mean not being able to react in time to repel a fast-approaching attack on a nearby village.

In the span of just a few months, a diverse group of major troop-contributing countries have endorsed the "Kigali Principles," including Rwanda, Ethiopia, Uganda, Senegal, Uruguay, the Netherlands, Italy, Sri Lanka, and Bangladesh. Already, one-third of all troops currently serving in U.N. and AU peacekeeping operations come from countries that have endorsed the "Kigali Principles"—and that proportion is rising. These principles are a new blueprint for peacekeepers—and especially infantry—deploying into volatile situations.

This growing clarity, together with the significant new contributions announced at the September summit, can change the impact that peacekeepers have in the field. In the past, the scant supply of troops and police meant that neither the U.N. nor the countries contributing the lion's share of peacekeepers could afford to be selective without leaving significant gaps in missions. However, the summit pledges of nearly 50,000 troops and police should enable more capable, more willing troops and police to staff peacekeeping missions. Troop- and police-contributing countries that have qualms with particular mandates, or doubts about their capacity to do what is asked of them, no longer need to deploy to missions simply because nobody else will.

For its part, the U.N. must demonstrate leadership by strengthening its monitoring and evaluation of troops and police in the field. When underperformance results from a lack of appropriate training and equipping, we must help to build those capabilities over time. When it is a matter of misconduct, refusal to follow commands, or implement mandated tasks, or take seriously the imperative to root out misconduct, particularly sexual exploitation and abuse, the U.N. must repatriate those responsible. For the first time in two decades, the surplus of troops and police allows the U.N. to do just that.

Fourth, we need to press the U.N. to make bold institutional reforms. Last year, the U.N. Secretary-General appointed a High-Level Independent Panel on U.N. Peace Operations to undertake a thorough review of U.N. peacekeeping and political missions. The Panel released an in-depth report that included reform recommendations, many of which align with long-standing U.S. priorities. In September, the Secretary-General released his report outlining his intentions to implement the Panel's recommendations ranging from improved logistics and sustainment through its Department of Field Support, to a more comprehensive approach to crisis situations that integrates military, police, and civilian tools.

The Administration is currently focused on several key areas of institutional reform.

We are working to strengthen the U.N.'s assessment and planning work, which includes: supporting the use of sequenced mandates; encouraging the review and revision of conflict analysis tools across the system; and, supporting improved assessment analysis and planning capabilities. Better analysis and planning and the sequencing of mandates not only help to tailor peace operations to better suit often dynamic contexts, but we predict could also result in cost savings. For example, more tailored peace operations could help ensure that the U.N. isn't being asked to deploy expensive state-capacity building components before a host-state government has the credibility or ability to absorb such support.

We are supporting efforts to enhance the U.N.'s ability to undertake strategic force generation and deploy rapidly. This is an area in dire need of improvement, as we have seen in the long lead times getting troops into Mali, CAR and South Sudan. Rapid deployment of peacekeeping missions can be critical to stabilizing crisis situations, yet we have seen continued shortfalls in staffing-up missions such as in the emergency surge the Security Council authorized for the mission in South Sudan. We must look at what structures and arrangements the U.N. needs to best support the rapid deployment of peacekeepers and equipment.

We are encouraging the Secretary-General and appropriate heads of U.N. departments and divisions to undertake administrative reform and cultural shifts that will empower the field and allow for flexibility and responsiveness. The U.N.'s ability to respond to needs in the field is hamstrung by burdensome policies and procedures and a culture overly concerned with compliance on paper versus outcomes in practice. Getting the right leadership is also critical for mission success. The U.N. can improve its selection process for senior mission leaders, including by prioritizing leadership and management skills, increasing commitments to gender diversity among qualified leaders, and developing meaningful mandatory training for senior leaders. The U.N. should also rigorously assess the performance of senior mission leaders and remove ineffective leaders when warranted. We are encouraging these efforts at the U.N. and working with the U.N. to enhance its training of senior mission leadership.

We also continue to support vigorously the Secretary-General's implementation of his zero tolerance policy on sexual exploitation and abuse (SEA). We have been particularly outraged at those especially egregious cases of SEA that have been reported in CAR, for example. Those who prey on the vulnerable communities they are sent to protect undermine the very foundation of peacekeeping. There is no excuse for inaction, and we must all do more to ensure those responsible for these heinous acts are held accountable.

I greatly appreciate the leadership you've shown on this issue, Mr. Chairman, and am fully aware of how important this issue is to the Committee. Like you, I believe that even a single case of SEA is one too many. The United States has long been a leader in pushing for stronger prevention measures, and concrete steps to ensure accountability for those responsible for SEA.

Despite the horrific incidents that have been recently reported, the U.N. has come a long way in recent years in responding to the scourge of SEA with strong support from the United States. However, there is a lot of work that still remains in preventing and addressing SEA. We remain concerned that many SEA perpetrators commit these acts, which are often crimes, with impunity and that many SEA victims never report such to the U.N.

In order to address this accountability gap, and to improve prevention measures and assistance to victims, the U.S. government is instituting a "full court press." We are working with our partners to ensure that the Secretary-General remains fully committed and empowered to implement this policy. At the President's Peacekeeping Summit at the U.N. in September, for example, 42 countries signed onto the Summit Declaration, which affirmed support for the Secretary-General's zero tolerance policy, and confirmed commitments to rigorous vetting and training of uniformed personnel, swift and thorough investigations, and appropriate accountability measures and timely reporting to the U.N. on all allegations.

Because we know that SEA is an issue that affects all member states, we are developing a whole-of-government strategy to improve prevention of SEA and enhance transparency and accountability for perpetrators. President Obama's recent memorandum on U.N. peacekeeping highlighted the importance of combatting SEA, and some of the initiatives that the U.S. government is undertaking.

To effectively combat SEA, we are working to track individual cases where there is information available, following up with the appropriate authorities, analyzing the strengths and weakness of current policies, and providing support or applying pressure as appropriate to the U.N. We are further exploring setting a requirement for rigorous pre-deployment training in the Secretary-General's zero tolerance policy on SEA. And, we will be highlighting instances of SEA in the annual human rights report. In addition to elevating incidents of SEA, these acts will pressure, incentivize, and enable troop- and police-contributing countries to better handle SEA.

Perhaps the greatest challenge in our efforts to eliminate SEA has been the lack of transparency on allegations. Although we need to ensure the appropriate procedures are followed and that privacy is respected for all those accused of SEA, the U.N. and Member States should know the nationality of alleged perpetrators, the status of investigations, and the outcome of disciplinary or prosecutorial action, or of sanctions imposed by the U.N. Unfortunately, we rarely have access to this type of information. Our initiatives with the U.N. have been largely focused on increasing transparency in this regard, specifically to ensure accountability. The lack of data has been very problematic, because it prevents us from following-up with governments and fully analyzing the factors that most contribute to SEA: whether it is a lack of discipline, cultures of tolerance within missions, or lack of training, as these all differ across troop- and police-contributing countries and across U.N. peacekeeping operations. It has also been difficult to track the U.N.'s follow up on specific cases, since in the past we have not known for sure what country is responsible.

We applaud the Secretary-General's commitment to publicizing the nationality of individuals against whom credible allegations of SEA have been made in his next annual report on this issue. This idea originated in the Secretary-General's 2012 report on SEA, where he noted his intention to "provide country-specific information on the number of credible allegations being investigated by Member States in reports to the General Assembly."

This information will better enable us to use our own diplomatic efforts to ensure accountability. Once we know which country's personnel have been accused of misconduct, we will have a much better understanding of the nature of the problem, the actual size of the accountability gap, and how to better target our response. In cases where countries have repeated SEA violations, we will be able to work bilaterally to address capacity issues and to encourage countries to take appropriate action.

We are also working with the U.N. to improve standard operating procedures for SEA prevention, reporting, and investigations. The Secretary-General has taken a strong stance and very decisive action on SEA. In response to repeated allegations of SEA in MINUSCA, the U.N.'s peacekeeping operation in the Central African Republic, he requested and accepted the resignation of his Special Representative Babacar Gaye in August of this year. His recent reports on SEA in peacekeeping outline very detailed steps he is taking under his own authority to address SEA. These include: community outreach strategies to increase awareness about SEA and reporting mechanisms; establishing Immediate Response Teams to preserve evidence following allegations; tighter timelines for SEA investigations; and, suspending payments to troop and police contributing countries in connection with individuals alleged to have committed SEA. We welcome the Secretary-General's leadership on SEA.

Finally, the United States continues to explore ways to support a more predictable and flexible funding mechanism to support AU peace operations, conditioned on increased AU financing and operational capacities, and compliance with U.N. regulations, rules, and policies, including financial rules, as well as with international humanitarian and human rights law, as applicable. These operations provide a creative and oftentimes cost-effective alternative to U.N. peacekeeping when environments are particularly volatile such as Somalia or early on in CAR.

U.S. Support for U.N. Peacekeeping

In order to fulfill the first goal outlined above—building partner capacity—the United States must continue to show leadership in supporting peacekeeping operations. Not only is this support good for peacekeeping, it also positions us to be maximally effective in driving changes that will strengthen peacekeeping, and deliver greater results from our investments.

As President Obama said in his remarks at the Summit, "We are here today, together, to strengthen and reform U.N. peacekeeping because our common security demands it. This is not something that we do for others; this is something that we do collectively because our collective security depends on it." In concert with the other Summit participants' pledges, President Obama announced his intention to significantly increase the number of U.S. personnel serving under the U.N. flag by working to double our contribution of military staff officers serving as individuals or teams in U.N. missions.

Additional U.S. commitments announced at the Summit are aimed at supporting U.N. peacekeeping in three key areas. First, to reduce response time and support rapid response, the United States is prepared to offer access to our unparalleled strategic air- and sealift capabilities to support U.N. deployments in crisis situations. Second, the United States is prepared to provide engineering support, an important enabler of U.N. operations and another comparative U.S. strength, which could include technical expertise and making available military engineers for specific projects on a project-by-project basis, where there is an urgent need that the United States is uniquely positioned to address. These units would remain under existing policies on U.S. command and control. Third, the United States plans to pre-position defense equipment to accelerate equipping and deployment of personnel to U.N. and regional peacekeeping operations, essential in crises. The United States will also factor U.N. and regional peacekeeping needs as a priority in determining which countries receive appropriate U.S. surplus defense equipment.

The United States will endeavor to increase its already substantial contributions to building the capacity of the U.N. and partner nations that contribute to peace operations in the following areas: in-mission training and mentoring, technology, leadership training, police pre-deployment training and counter-IED training and assessment.

For example, the United States is committing to make available mobile training teams on a case-by-case basis for deployment alongside partners who are contributing forces and deploying into a peace operation. U.S. personnel plan to work directly with U.N. experts to identify cost-effective technology solutions for needs in countering IEDs, force protection, protection of civilians, collaborative planning, information-led operations, rapid deployment of vanguard forces, and expeditionary logistics. The United States intends to increase its already significant contributions to U.N. police in peacekeeping by allocating another $2 million—subject to congressional notification—to develop and expand the capability of African partners deploying police personnel, specifically to enhance their ability to meet the challenges of violent extremism in missions such as the one in Mali. The United States is also contributing $2 million specifically for counter-IED training and intends to offer to deploy U.S. military counter-IED specialists to conduct strategic and operational-level assessments alongside select U.N. peacekeeping operations. Importantly, these commitments will not require the budgeting of additional funds, as they are all either reimbursable by the U.N. or funded within existing programs.

In addition, through the GPOI program, the United States is currently helping 50 partner countries and three regional organizations build the capacity to deploy to and effectively perform in U.N. peacekeeping missions. The GPOI model builds partner countries' training self-sufficiency and supports the development of critically needed enabling capabilities—such as lift, logistics, and medical units. Program activities not only address the short-term requirement of providing capable troops to missions but also provide a lasting foundation to support the peacekeeping needs of the future.

Conclusion

Although we remain focused on the unique opportunity for reform in 2016 and beyond, we should not forget that U.N. peacekeeping is stronger than it was two decades ago. The U.N. has improved logistics and sustainment through its Department of Field Support by modernizing its supply chain and asset management systems; it has strengthened lines of communication with headquarters; it has created an inspector-general function to evaluate candidly the U.N.'s performance; it has introduced a capabilities-based reimbursement system for troops; and it has developed a far more integrated approach to crisis situations, drawing on military, police, and civilian tools.

In closing, let me reflect on the budget. The lines of effort I have just described are all critical to ensuring peacekeeping better addresses 21st century challenges. They demonstrate the need for U.S. leadership. And to exercise that leadership, the United States must pay our U.N. dues in full and on time.

I understand the frustration that many Americans feel with the United States paying a substantial share of the U.N.'s peacekeeping and regular budgets. We agree that the formula should be changed to reflect the realities of today's world. But, until that happens, if we suggest we should pay less and withhold our full dues at this critical moment, we will not only go against our commitments, but we will also dramatically undercut our ability to achieve needed reforms, undermine our leadership and erode our credibility with partners.

This does not mean we should simply sign over a large check and look the other way. On the contrary, as diligent stewards of taxpayer funds, over the last six years, we have pressed hard to improve the cost-efficiency of peacekeeping and to prevent significant new costs. Through U.S.-led reform efforts, the U.N. has cut the cost per-peacekeeper by roughly 17 percent—that's one-sixth of the cost reduced through efficiencies and streamlining. We have also aggressively fought cost increases, saving hundreds of millions of dollars per year by prevailing on other countries for a more modest increase in the long-frozen reimbursement rate for U.N. peacekeepers. And we have pressed to streamline and right-size missions where warranted by changing conditions on the ground. In the Ivory Coast, we have cut the number of mandated troops in half, from around 10,000 to 5,000. In Haiti, we have reduced the number of mandated troops from nearly 9,000 after the 2010 earthquake to just over 2,000 today. We were on course to do the same in Liberia prior to the outbreak of Ebola. These efforts ensure governments do not use peacekeepers as an excuse not to take responsibility for their citizens' own security. And streamlining missions frees up troops and resources that are needed elsewhere.

When the stakes are as high as they are in these conflicts—when shortfalls can result in atrocities committed, communities uprooted, and entire societies split along ethnic or religious lines—getting it right some of the time is not good enough. Peacekeeping must be consistently outstanding. We will keep working with our partners to bring about the kind of reforms upon which the security of millions of people around the world may depend. And we will continue to work relentlessly to make peacekeeping as efficient as possible without undermining its effectiveness, in close coordination with the Congress and especially this critically important Committee. Thank you.

The CHAIRMAN. Well, thank you very much for those comments.

Senator Isakson and I were in Darfur years ago and just infuriated by the caveats that the U.N. peacekeepers had. They could only fire at people when they were fired upon. You had women going out and collecting wood from their villages being raped, abused, people being murdered by the Janjaweed. Yet those caveats remained.

So we have evolved, as you mentioned. This is not our father's peacekeeping mission anymore.

As we have evolved these missions, though, and people now are placing themselves as peacekeepers more in the center of conflicts, in some cases taking sides, how has this changed the way the U.N. is viewed in these peacekeeping missions? I assume you believe this is in our national interests for us to be in these missions certainly, I do. But how has this changed the way these blue hats are viewed in these areas?

Ambassador POWER. Thank you, Senator Corker. It is an excellent question.

I think one of the lines that the U.N. struggles to walk is that it has, on the one hand, peacekeepers that are charged with an aggressive enforcement of mandates, which entail protecting civilians, not just protecting peacekeepers themselves, as was once the case. You have that on one hand. Then you have U.N. country programs that often look indistinguishable. They are all driving around in white vehicles, unarmed, passing out food, providing shelter, trying to provide counseling to those who have been victimized by sexual abuse.

So it has been challenging, the blurring of functions across these missions. But the only thing worse than confronting that challenge of having people in society distinguish who does what, is actually people in these societies rely on peacekeepers, know that the mandate says protect civilians, and have those peacekeepers bunkered and more interested, again, in collecting a paycheck and then going home than actually being out and about and delivering on the promise of that blue flag.

So, again, it varies per conflict area. I think we have come a long way. But as I noted, the statistics are not inspiring. I mean, there are still many troop-contributing countries who send their troops in without the very strict guidance that you will be sent home if you do not enforce the mandate you are given.

The CHAIRMAN. Yes. I appreciate the comment Senator Cardin made about the cost. But, as I understand it, for some of these countries, even though the cost to us is far less than having U.S. soldiers there, the pay for these soldiers is far greater than they would otherwise receive in their own countries. And, actually, if I understand correctly, that money goes to the national governments of those countries. And so these countries are benefiting financially in sending troops there.

Is that correct, in some cases, in some of the lower income countries? And is that feeding this situation of actually having troops there that are not, if you will, carrying out their mandates in an appropriate way, with soldiers not qualified or trained and not properly equipped? Talk to us a little bit about what is driving having folks within the peacekeeping missions that are that are certainly not conducting themselves in a professional manner.

Ambassador POWER. Well, thank you, Mr. Chairman, again. It reflects a real understanding of the dynamics in some of these missions.

Again, the performance is uneven. The motivation is uneven. The incentive for troops is uneven. If you take, for instance, Rwandan peacekeepers, who do get a more substantial stipend by serving in peacekeeping missions than they might if they were at home, but they are totally driven by what happened in their country 21 years ago and actually view protecting civilians as a way of showing the world what should have been done when the genocide unfolded in Rwanda.

Contrast that with other troops, again, who institutionally are not given the guidance from capital that they need to be out and about, that, yes, there are risks entailed with patrolling, but there are risks also that are entailed by being bunkered.

I think on the question, the very specific question of the stipend, as Senator Cardin said, this is a very good deal for the American taxpayer. These are extremely difficult environments, not only because of the risks of militia and government forces targeting peacekeepers as they are out and about, but also just the conditions in terms of logistics, access to water. I mean, these are missions that are not expending resources in the manner that our missions do when they deploy internationally. The logistic tail is not nearly as fulsome.

So I think it is important to incentivize their participation. Some countries are doing it because they are able, again, to secure additional resources that they are investing in ways that sometimes we do not have full visibility into, sometimes in professionalizing their militaries, sometimes in other parts of their government.

But I think Senator Cardin's point is very, very important. We are getting a lot out of the 100,000-plus troops who are active in these conflict areas. These are places where, in some instances, if you look at Mali or Lebanon, places that are really cutting-edge theaters in terms of terrorism and extremism, and if it weren't for

U.N. peacekeepers who were there putting their lives at risk, it may come to the United States at some point in order for us to advance our security.

The CHAIRMAN. As it relates to the issues of the abuse that has taken place that is, obviously, abhorrent, in fairness, I think people on both sides of the aisle have concerns about the U.N.'s ability to actually put reforms in place. And we understand how the U.N. operates, and I know you talked about the leader's desire to create reforms. We sent a letter suggesting that we have onsite court marshals by the countries to handle peacekeeping soldiers accused of crimes be tried, by the way, under their own country military preocedures to reduce impunity. We also made some other suggestions.

What is your sense that those types of reforms can be implemented, relative to peacekeeping?

Ambassador POWER. Well, as Ambassador Negroponte behind me I think will attest, through the life of the U.N. you have a challenge, always, on reform, in the sense that there are two places you have to secure—will and follow-through.

The first is with the countries that comprise the U.N. So every troop-contributing country to peacekeeping has to be prepared to look at the kinds of ideas that you put in your letter that we have been pushing in new York and implement in their own military changes to ensure follow-though, oversight in the first instance, follow-through on investigation, and accountability, whether a court martial or some kind of prosecution in civilian court.

And again, there is probably no one-size-fits-all solution, because every country has its own set of procedures, again, for following up on abuse of any kind.

Then there is the U.N. itself, which has to be much aggressive in shining a spotlight on those countries that are not taking the steps that are needed.

I think that we have seen improvements. This is, again, not something one should cite as an improvement. It should never have been the case that it was otherwise. But those individuals who were alleged to be involved in sexual abuse now are not being paid by the U.N. They are being recalled to their capital. Training and vetting now is changing, so that there is training on preventing sexual abuse and exploitation.

You had an idea, I believe, in your letter about a claims kind of commission. I think the U.N. is looking at creating a victim support trust fund, which is something, of course, we would wish to support as well. It is going to require going back to member states and getting resources to put into that, but maybe some of the docked pay of those against whom there are allegations could be used in service of such a fund. And then I think having more aggressive onsite investigative capacity, so that less time passes between an allegation and an actual follow-through.

Lastly, the two aspects of reform come together. In order to secure meaningful reform that actually matters for potential victims or people who have already been victimized, there has to be more transparency between what is actually going on in the field and then what we are made aware of in New York.

Too often, we hear from NGOs or from journalists about sexual abuse and exploitation, rather than from the U.N. itself. And if we are to go to a developing country and try to enhance their capacity, their training on the front end, their capacity to investigate on the backend of an allegation, we have to know who has been accused of doing what at what period, and be in a position to offer support.

If there are countries who are shirking their obligation to carry out investigations, we have to know so that we can look at our bilateral leverage and whether we might suspend some forms of assistance, if, in fact, there is a recurrent pattern of not actually taking seriously the zero-tolerance policy.

The CHAIRMAN. Well, thank you. My time is up. And as a courtesy, I want to move on.

I do hope through questioning at some point and—I know the President has made additional pledges to the U.N. beyond our normal peacekeeping budgeting. I hope at some point it will come to light as to where those resources are planned to come from. But thank you again for being here.

Senator Cardin?

Senator CARDIN. Thank you, Mr. Chairman.

And thank you, Ambassador Power, for your service to our country.

As I said in my opening statement, I am a strong supporter of the mission of the United Nations and the incredible progress it has made in global issues. I want to talk about transparency and accountability. It has come up quite a bit on several subjects.

One of the, I think, clearest ways to try to help the safety of civilians is to hold President Assad of Syria accountable for violating international war-crime-type activities. So do we have your commitment, as our Ambassador in the United Nations, that we will seek full accountability by President Assad for the war crimes that he has committed in any of these negotiations that take place in regard to the resolution of Syria?

Ambassador POWER. Thank you, Senator.

Well, let me say that one of my more unsuccessful days in my office, since this body was good enough to confirm me for my job, was pursuing a referral of the war crimes and crimes against humanity carried out in Syria to the International Criminal Court. That was a resolution we brought to the U.N. Security Council. Notwithstanding our own nonparticipation in the ICC, we believe that is a venue that should be looking at chemical weapons attacks and barrel-bomb attacks and systematic torture. And, of course, that effort at a referral was vetoed by Russia, a veto supported by China.

Senator CARDIN. I do understand there are going to be negotiations that will involve the United States. And the United States is going to have to sign off on those negotiations. Do I have your commitment that your position at the United Nations will be to hold President Assad accountable for the type of activities you just described?

Ambassador POWER. The ultimate settlement in Syria is going to be between the opposition and the Syrian Government. The United States position on accountability I hope is well-known. We are absolutely supportive and have been aggressively supportive in building an evidentiary base so as to ensure that Assad and other people responsible for war crimes are held accountable.

Senator CARDIN. It is not up to the government and opposition to determine whether a person has violated international standards on conduct of war. War crimes are global. It is global accountability.

Ambassador POWER. I think there are two separate issues. One is what is the standard or the threshold question for where accountability should be provided or whether prosecution or a truth commission, the whole set of tactical question about how accountability should be pursued.

There is a related, overlapping question of what the terms of a political settlement would be. I mean, this is not something that is on the verge of happening, so I think the details on accountability have not yet been fleshed out, and it is something we should consult on.

But I want to underscore that the final agreement has to be something that both the opposition and the government can get behind.

Senator CARDIN. I understand that. It does not quite answer my question.

Let me make my position clear, and I think the members of this committee. If President Assad is not held accountable, there will not be support for any solution in regard to Syria. I will just make that pretty clear from the beginning.

Let me talk to issue number two on transparency and accountability. The chairman has already talked about that, the abuse allegations. If this is not done in an open manner, where there is complete understanding and disclosure of what is taking place, the confidence factor of those responsible for these abuses being held accountable will not be there.

Ambassador POWER. I agree completely. I mean, I am not sure what to add.

As I said, there has been insufficient reporting back to the Security Council. We have now taken sexual abuse and exploitation and made it an issue to be discussed in the Security Council. The Secretary General has now committed to reporting back.

Senator CARDIN. And I have seen the specific recommendations, and they are good. But you have to follow through on it, and it has to be done in a way that the international community, the activists, those who are following this, can be confident that those who are responsible have truly been held accountable, so that this will not happen in the future, will not be tolerated in the future. You said zero tolerance, which we agree.

That is, I think, the important point, that it is not just a closed investigation, but that we have an open closure of this issue and a commitment on how to go forward on how these matters will be handled.

Ambassador POWER. I think right now, Senator, it is very fair to say that victims who come forward do so at their own peril, and do not do so with confidence that having taken that risk, having potentially ostracized themselves in their own communities, that there is even going to be accountability on the backend. That has to change entirely. I suspect if it does change, you may well see more people coming forward.

Senator CARDIN. So let me get to my third point on transparency and accountability, and that is the budget system at the United Nations. It is anything but open and clear and transparent. That is nothing new. It has been that way for a long time.

It is hard for me to understand why our assessment on the peacekeeping is 28.36 percent, if I am correct, which is almost three times higher than the next country and is significantly higher than our general allocation for the U.N. budget.

That does not seem to me to be a transparent way to budget. So can you just briefly inform us as to the U.S. position in regard to a fair allocation of the U.N. budget in an open and transparent manner?

Ambassador POWER. Thank you, Senator.

The formula on the U.S. share of the peacekeeping budget is a very complex formula. Let me say in brief that it is some combination of our share of the global economy plus a premium that we pay by being a permanent member of the Security Council and, particularly with the veto, getting to dictate whether a mission comes into existence or whether it does not, along with the other permanent members as a whole, along with the rest of the Security Council. So we pay a premium for being a permanent member.

We were able to secure the cap on our regular budget. The formula would actually have us pay at a higher rate if not for the 22 percent cap that Ambassador Holbrooke secured now going on 15 years ago.

The one thing I want to stress is that our emphasis is on ensuring that countries that are contributing more and more to the global economy are paying more of their share. We are in the midst of scales negotiations now on our share of the peacekeeping budget. Our emphasis, again, has been on ensuring countries, you can see their economic growth, but you do not see a correlation in terms of their contribution.

The Chinese contribution to peacekeeping has more than doubled in the last 10 years. And I think we can anticipate that the Chinese share is going to be up around 10 percent, which would be a tripling of its share. Similarly, the Russian contribution has doubled. Again, China and Russia being two of the five permanent members on the council.

Senator CARDIN. Well, we should point out that China is still about one-fourth of the United States, less than one-fourth. And Russia is about one-eighth of the United States.

It just seems to us that that 22 percent cap, we understand that and that was well-deserved, the way that came out. It looks like the United Nations is equalizing through the peacekeeping percentage and that the 22 percent cap is being violated because of our higher contributions to the peacekeeping efforts.

I just urge you that the more transparent this process, the better it is going to be, I think, received politically in our country. And we do think the 22 percent is a fair number. We think it should be honored and be honored in the peacekeeping.

Ambassador POWER. I just want to underscore that when the agreement was secured on the 22 percent cap, no similar agreement was secured as it related to peacekeeping. In fact, having the 22 percent cap actually helps us in the peacekeeping realm because 22 percent becomes the baseline on which these premiums are agreed to.

I want to stress, we share the same objective. We want to get other countries to step up and pay their share. We still believe that if you look, again, at what this means for U.S. national security—I think this is, again, a version of the argument you made at the beginning—that even when you compare it to NATO, where the United States bears the lion's share of defense investments, that having the rest of the world paying 72 percent of the peacekeeping budget is a good deal for the American taxpayer.

Senator CARDIN. And my last point and I hope this will be covered, as the chairman said, by others, the safety of civilians is critically important. You stressed the increased number commitment made in the meeting in September.

It seems to me it is not a matter of numbers of personnel. Do they have the will to go in and stand in front of civilians to protect them? We have not seen that.

So I am not sure I was comforted by your reply that we have greater capacity by number. If we do not have greater capacity by will, the civilian population is going to be at great risk.

Ambassador POWER. If I may, Senator, just respond briefly.

The point that I emphasized in my testimony was that we have succeeded now in getting contributions, or commitments, I should say, not yet contributions, from advanced militaries.

Europe had gotten out of peacekeeping, by and large, over the course of the last 20 years, and we think it is really important that they get back in. There is no necessary correlation always between being an advanced military and having the political will to put yourself in harm's way to protect civilians.

But we think that, again, giving the U.N. the choice—now it has a pool from which it can choose. And if there are people who show insufficient will and want to spend more time in their bases than out and about protecting civilians, we think having this pool of forces, which include, again, more professional and advanced militaries and better aviation and engineering and infantry capabilities, giving the U.N. that selectivity is going to mean over time that the performance of these peacekeepers is going to improve.

So numbers alone do not mean anything, if you have 50,000 commitments of people who do not have political will. But we see in that pool, actually, substantial commitments from those we think do have that will.

The CHAIRMAN. Before turning to Senator Perdue, I just want to thank the ranking member for bringing up an issue that is brought up consistently, certainly, on our side of the aisle. I want to thank him for that.

I do want to just emphasize that with NATO, which I know is not in your jurisdiction, we have become the provider of security services. Our NATO allies, generally speaking, are the consumer of security services.

And the same thing is happening with peacekeeping at the U.N. I know it is a different set of actors.

But the very people that stymie our efforts to pursue our interests—China, for instance—are taking advantage of us with respect to sharing the peacekeeping costs. So yes, it is in our U.S. national interests that we have peacekeeping missions and that we have stability and security around the world. But I think we continue to be not as good as we should be at forcing other nations to also be responsible.

So I want to thank Senator Cardin for bringing this important issue up. It is infuriating—infuriating—to have the lack of transparency that exists at the U.N. I think, over time, it will erode support. Such support is already not particularly high because of the many issues we see going unattended, like not dealing with the ballistic missiles that are being fired by Iran in violation of UNSCR 1929.

So I would just say, I am glad there is bipartisan concern. I hope that you can address it.

With that, Senator Perdue.

Senator PERDUE. Thank you, Mr. Chairman.

Let me also echo that. I want to compliment the ranking member for continuing to bring this up. I wanted to talk about that just in a second.

Right now, we are spending about $2 billion just in the peacekeeping force for the United States. I think that is our contribution. Because of the assessment disagreement, we are some $345 million in arrears, I think, in terms of what the U.N. says we owe them.

I would like to point out also, Mr. Chairman, that it is not just the percentages here in relation to the size of the GDP. Also, I think, it should be taken into account the percentage of GDPs in these countries that are spent on their own military. That also bears to the global security situation.

So I think given the situation we have the in the U.S., Madam Ambassador, in the last few years, 35 percent to 40 percent of what we have been spending is borrowed, I think this is a very timely time to have that really serious conversation in the U.N. I applaud you guys for doing that.

I have two quick questions.

First, I want to thank you for what you are doing. Given your high school years in Georgia, we claim you and we are proud of what you are doing.

So I want to talk about Hezbollah, and I want to talk about Lebanon in just a minute.

You know, in 1978, UNIFIL was created there as the interim force in Lebanon. Some 12,000 troops are there from the U.N. Resolution 1701 in 2006 strengthened the mandate there to monitor and to preclude the illegal transport of weapons into Lebanon. And yet we know today they have an estimated 120,000, 150,000 rockets, some of these very sophisticated guided weapons. It is very troubling.

So it looks to me like, if that mandate was directed to keep weapons out of Lebanon, they are failing against that mandate.

Can you talk a little bit about their current role there? And what is their role against 1701? And then we have had reports that there have been threats around reprisals if they report violations and so forth. What can we do to strengthen UNIFIL there and to preclude Lebanon from the illegal transport of these dangerous weapons?

Ambassador POWER. Thank you.

UNIFIL has, I think, played an ameliorative role since 2006 in calming the situation, but there is no question that Hezbollah has been able to maintain and expand an arsenal. And we have and continue to urge UNIFIL to be more aggressive in patrolling, in monitoring, in speaking out about violations of the UNIFIL mandate.

And I think that what you have seen, actually, in recent months is at least more transparency on the part of UNIFIL. I mean, part of the challenge here is, as we know from confronting terrorist organizations in other parts of the world, when you are not at war with those terrorist organizations, you are using political pressure, particularly by Lebanon's own sovereign institutions, which are themselves very weak, as we know from the current paralysis in Lebanon. You are shining a spotlight. You are trying to ensure interdiction of weapons before they even get into the theater in question.

So UNIFIL is not a perfect fix for everything that ails Lebanon or for the threat posed by Hezbollah. But it has a responsibility to be vocal and to take very seriously its reporting mandate, also so countries in the region, including our friends, know what is happening in an area from which threats have come routinely in recent decades.

Senator PERDUE. Also, let me just ask you to add a comment or two about Syria. The U.N. Disengagement Observer Force, UNDOF, has actually withdrawn from the Golan on the Syrian side, because of the fighting there. Can you speak to their role now? And how are they interacting with IDF in that?

And I have one last question.

Ambassador POWER. Thank you.

I mean, you are right that there has been a reconfiguration. This is something UNDOF has done in close consultation with the Government of Israel. Given the stakes here, it is a response to the fact that al-Nusra made advances on one side of the line. And right now this is——

Senator PERDUE. They actually kidnapped some of the U.N. forces.

Ambassador POWER. Exactly, Senator, they did. And the release of those forces had to be negotiated.

And I will say, even that incident showed, it is not the same as civilian protection, but an unevenness in how the different units responded, which again is life in the U.N. Some holding onto their weapons, refusing to be cowed. Others handing over their weapons and, unfortunately, in a manner that left UNDOF weaker and where those weapons had to be replenished.

But we again view this as a temporary relocation. We still believe the prior configuration is the stabilizing configuration. But I think the Israelis are well-aware as well that the circumstances do not lend themselves to putting the observers on the other side of the line.

Senator PERDUE. The last question I have with the time remaining, Ambassador, the chairman mentioned it, is on the violations of Iran. We have been concerned since the JCPOA that Iran would violate our agreement incrementally. They are violating the U.N. agreement not incrementally, but in a major way—these are Resolutions 1929 and 2231—with the launch in October. And then we have reports in the last week or so of a second launch.

What is the U.N. doing in relation to those violations and the sanctions that back those up?

Ambassador POWER. Thank you, Senator. Yes, this is something that I have had occasion to talk to the chairman about. And it is music to a U.N. Ambassador's ears when Resolution 1929, Resolution 2231 just roll off the tongue of Members of Congress.

Resolution 1929 has been an incredibly important foundation to the international sanctions regime. The ballistic missile launch from October is a violation of 1929. As soon as we confirmed the launch, we brought it to the Security Council. We now are going to be discussing it on Tuesday. The U.N. machinery always works slowly.

The panel of experts is looking at it. We have provided all the information that we have on it.

And, in a way, the Security Council is an important venue for increasing the political costs on Iran when they violate Resolution 1929.

I would note, of course, that the JCPOA is aimed at dismantling Iran's nuclear weapons program, so that the threat that Iran poses in any aspect of its military is much diminished.

The Security Council sanctions body operates by consensus. This is something that over time benefits the United States. But on something like that, it means we have to convince all members of the committee also to support our desired designations or any further form of accountability.

Senator PERDUE. So what is the U.S. trying to move forward in terms of strengthening the sanctions?

Ambassador POWER. Well, it is the U.N. machinery. We have to get the report back from the panel of experts. We will discuss it in the committee. And then we will look at what the right tool is.

I think it is very important, also, to look at the bilateral tools we have. We maintain sanctions, as you know, and will, even after implementation day, on ballistic missiles, on counterterrorism, on human rights. And I think we many of the individuals involved in their ballistic missile program have already been sanctioned, as you well know, over the years. So trying to secure a nexus between this launch and any particular individual entity is a challenge that we need to take on.

But I think looking at the Security Council and our bilateral tools as complementary is very important in this regard.

Senator PERDUE. Thank you. Thank you again for your service.

Ambassador POWER. Thank you, Senator.

The CHAIRMAN. Thank you.

Senator Cardin and I both emphasized with the Security Council 2 days ago that, look, let us face it. The possible military dimensions piece, we thought they might get a D-. They got an F. A total hoax. A total hoax.

Non-action here is just going to empower them to continue to violate. And I think what the Ambassador just said is the U.N. is going to do nothing—nothing—because China and Russia will block that from occurring.

So I do hope they are preparing their bilateral efforts.

It is disappointing that, again, we provide the resources that we do, and yet we have countries that will not cause other countries to live up to their obligations and block that. So it is very disappointing.

Senator Coons?

Senator COONS. Thank you, Chairman Corker and Ranking Member Cardin.

And thank you, Ambassador Power, for your tireless and dedicated service, your advocacy for human rights, your leadership in representing us at the United Nations, and your passion for the difficult and demanding mission that you are carrying out on behalf of our Nation.

I share the concerns expressed by many colleagues about the active enforcement of the JCPOA and ongoing work to enforce U.N. Security Council resolutions.

I was pleased to hear there is an upcoming meeting of finance ministers around the U.N. Security Council and look forward to continuing to work closely with you and Secretary Lew and others in the administration to make sure that we are using all the tools we can to enforce the sanctions that remain in place and to re-impose sanctions, should Iranian behavior demonstrate the necessity of doing so.

I have had the opportunity to visit U.N. peacekeepers in the field in a number countries, and have seen both the positive that they can accomplish in countries like Liberia and the DRC, and some of the very real challenges, particularly where, as you noted in your opening testimony, there is a disconnect between the mission to protect civilians and the training equipment, leadership, and inclination or will to do so.

So start, if you would, by just focusing on whether there is a mismatch between U.N. Security Council mandates and what troop-contributor countries are really trained and prepared to do.

I was very encouraged by the President's leadership in renewing a call to more advanced militaries to deliver not just logistics and intelligence and supplies, but trainers and troops.

How do we connect the mandates, the mission, and the capacity to deliver in the field?

Ambassador POWER. Thank you, Senator.

Let me come back, maybe if I could, just by way of response to something Senator Corker mentioned before, which is the contrast with NATO. I mean, I just want to underscore this really is an example where we have national security interests in peacekeepers, in troops from other countries, performing ably. This is not a NATO situation where we are carrying a disproportionate share of the troop burden. We are carrying a large share of the financial burden. And that is something, again, we are working to ensure is allocated more fairly.

I think on the mandate troop-contributor disconnect, which is real, and I think it is real across the board, the first thing you have to do is get more quality troops. It has been, as you know well, a supply-driven market insofar as the U.N. basically goes begging bowl in hand to different countries. There is no standing army that exists in New York. The Secretary General does not have anything at his disposal beyond what he can extract from U.N. member states.

That process had yielded a very uneven set of troops and police to participate in these missions, some who have extensive military experience at home and we know are capable troops, but once they get in a peacekeeping setting, they do not fundamentally believe in a civilian protection mandate. They want to go back to traditional principles of peacekeeping, the way peacekeeping was done back in the 1970s and 1980s. And that is just not the world we are in.

So I think the first answer is you increase the sophistication, the training, the professionalization of the troops, and there is going to be an effect on the ability to perform the mandates.

But the second answer is on us, as a permanent member of the Security Council, which is, there needs to be more prioritization in the way that these mandates are put in place. It is hard in the real world to prioritize, because you look at a situation like that in South Sudan or that in Congo, and what of the tasks that those peacekeepers are slated to perform would you give up? Would you give up demobilization? Would you give up security sector reform? Would you give up human rights monitoring? Would you give up attention to child soldiers or sexual violence? Of course not.

So you need to make sure that the missions are right-sized. You need, maybe, to do some sequencing in terms of building out some of those capabilities over time. And the U.N. country team and our bilateral assistance also needs to be involved in strengthening state institutions, because fundamentally whether it is the Central African Republic or eastern Congo or South Sudan, U.N. peacekeepers de facto are having to perform the work of states, because the states themselves are so weak.

And so, again, there is no panacea. And for all of the complaints that we have about U.N. peacekeeping, I would challenge all of us to imagine what any one of those countries would be like without this somewhat stabilizing presence. But it is not going to be a cure-all for as long as you have state institutions that do not function, or leaders that are corrupt, or militia on the loose who are interested in carrying out horrors against their civilians.

Senator COONS. I have seen exactly those challenges in the countries I referenced, among others. So I continue as an appropriator to advocate for funding peacekeeping and for dealing with some of these challenges. So it is very encouraging for me to see your engagement and hard work on reform, because for this to be cost-effective and yet reflect our values, we need to make some real progress in the areas around accountability and protection of civilians that you have referenced.

Let me just ask sort of a last question and then take what time you have left to answer. I am concerned about sort of growing the universe of capable peacekeepers, both in Africa and globally. China made a pledge of a standby force of 8,000 peacekeepers, and I am interested in what you think is the future, where they will or will not be deployed, what this commitment means. And I am concerned about the African Union and A–Prep, and would love to hear how you see that playing out going forward, and how we can sustain that investment in a continent-wide force.

Ambassador POWER. Thank you.

Well, again, I just want to stress how unusual President Obama's personal leadership on this has been. And he has basically told us that anything he can do to ensure that these commitments are followed through on, he is prepared to invest his own time, and the Vice President the same.

So we are dealing with a set of challenges at a level that I do not think we have seen before, and with a degree of aggressiveness that we have not seen before from the United States, notwithstanding the fact that, again, on a bipartisan basis I think successive administrations have seen the value of this tool in the American and multilateral toolbox.

I think that the A–Prep and the China question kind of come together a little bit. We have a major issue in terms of the delay between the time a mandate is given a U.N. peacekeeping force and the time in which troops and police are deployed into theater.

Now again, some of this just goes back to the troop-contributing countries and their ability to turn on a dime, and train, and get configured, and get their equipment all lined up.

A–Prep is designed to take the six militaries, all of whom are have a good record within peacekeeping of being aggressive in protecting civilians and having the political will to go to dangerous places, and we aim to then ensure through deepening our provision of equipment and the particular forms of training we offer, that they can get into the theater more quickly than they have been up to this point. A lot of them lack their own ability to lift themselves, so sometimes we have to be involved, as we were in the Central African Republic for the Burundians and Rwandans, to swoop in and actually carry people into harm's way. But they need to acquire, over time, the lift and the self-sustainment, and, again, this ability to if not be formally on standby, to be ready to go when the 911 comes.

China's commitment of 8,000 troops is a very large piece of business and was a very significant announcement out of President Obama's summit. I do not think we, yet, have a sense, nor does the U.N., of how they imagine allocating that set of forces over time.

Right now, they have just deployed their first infantry battalion ever, and that is in South Sudan. The reports are quite promising in terms of how active those troops are, out and about, but also protecting civilians in the displaced person camps.

So we need to look and see how the U.N. chooses to use that commitment.

Rapid response, if that were something that China could put on offer, where you could actually lose less time between the time the international community comes together with a consensus that a mission is needed and the time when troops show up. I mean, in South Sudan we are 2 years after the original deployment, and they are still not at full troop strength. And that is a recurring pattern. So we would welcome rapid response.

Of course, we also need to make sure that any peacekeeper that deploys has the mindset where they are willing to protect civilians and put themselves at risk for the sake of the mandate.

Senator COONS. Thank you, Madam Ambassador.

Thank you, Chairman.

The CHAIRMAN. Thank you.

Senator Gardner?

Senator GARDNER. Thank you, Mr. Chairman.

And thank you, Madam Ambassador, for your time and testimony today. And, of course, thank you as well for your service to this country.

I want to follow up a little bit on what Chairman Corker and Senator Perdue were asking about, and that is Security Council Resolutions 1929 and 2231. Of course, we know there was a second ballistic missile test from Iran, which was a clear violation of these resolutions.

After the first launch in October, we referred, as you said, the matter to the United Nations, and called on it to "review this matter quickly and recommend appropriate action." On October 22, I believe you stated, and I quote, "The United States will continue to press the Security Council to respond effectively to any future violations of U.N. Security Council resolutions. Full and robust enforcement of all relevant U.N. measures is and will remain critical."

So as of today, has the United Nations Security Council or sanctions committee taken any actions in response to the Iranian missile test? And I believe the answer is, no, they are meeting Tuesday. Is that correct?

Ambassador POWER. Yes. Beyond having Security Council discussions of the matter, there has been no follow-on action. Discussions are a form of U.N. action. It is a little bit like hearing is a form of congressional action. So we have had multiple discussions.

Senator GARDNER. The Tuesday meeting, can you describe the actions that will be taken in that Tuesday meeting?

Ambassador POWER. We will hear back. Well, we will actually probably not yet hear back from the panel of experts. But if we are in a position to confirm the recent launch, this is something that we would bring to the council. We are not yet in a position to confirm, but are looking to confirm those reports, if warranted.

And again, we will get an update from the U.N. in terms of when the panel of experts' report is going to come back.

Senator GARDNER. And so this launch needs to be confirmed, but the last launch, we still have not taken any action on the last launch?

Ambassador POWER. Again, we have taken action.

Senator GARDNER. What are those actions?

Ambassador POWER. We confirmed the violation. We brought it to the U.N. Security Council, and the panel of experts is investigating the matter and will report back.

Senator GARDNER. So what other actions has the administration taken in response to the missile test, other than taking it to the panel, talking about it, and having a meeting?

Ambassador POWER. We are looking also, as I mentioned earlier, at the bilateral sanctions tools that we have at our disposal. So that is something, again, that the Treasury Department is following up on.

Senator GARDNER. What unilateral measures are we considering?

Ambassador POWER. I believe sanctions designations, bearing in mind that that most actors—I shouldn't say "most"—many of the actors involved in ballistic missile launches in the program itself are already sanctioned under U.S. law.

Senator GARDNER. And are we considering stopping sanctions relief from proceeding or rescinded any previous relief, as a result of these actions?

Ambassador POWER. The JCPOA, as you know, the sanctions relief associated with the JCPOA, will not occur until after the initial steps have been taken and the IAEA has verified that those initial nuclear-related steps are taken.

But I want to underscore, again, that the point of the JCPOA is to dismantle Iran's nuclear weapons program, and that is a really important area of emphasis for us.

Senator GARDNER. So more important than the ballistic missile concerns?

Ambassador POWER. I do not want to talk about relative importance, but taking away Iran's—I think this is something all of us can agree upon—actually ensuring that Iran does not develop a nuclear weapon is a huge priority.

Senator GARDNER. You mentioned in your opening statement, you said, and I quote, "exploit vacuum of authority." I think you were referring to actors in the Middle East and other terrorists, that they were maybe trying to exploit a vacuum of authority.

By not imposing sanctions, by not designating individuals, by not doing anything other than talking, are we not allowing exploitation of a vacuum of authority?

Ambassador POWER. This administration has put in place, in the case of the Iran sanctions regime, as you know, this body, the Congress, in the first instance, and then amplified and extended by what we have done at the U.N., the most devastating sanctions regime in the 70-year history of the United Nations.

So I do not think there is a void or a vacuum. Iran has seen the consequences of violating international norms. We also have a sanction snapback provision that I think few around the world would have thought we could have secured as part of this deal, which would allow any single country to snap back in the event of significant noncompliance with the deal.

So sanctions are a really important tool. The sanctions that this Congress has put in place is one reason we are in the position we are now to ensure that Iran does not develop a nuclear weapon.

Senator GARDNER. But nothing has been done, other than a meeting coming up on Tuesday with a panel of experts on a ballistic missile violation.

Ambassador POWER. We have increased, and will continue to increase, the political cost to Iran when it violates U.N. Security Council resolutions.

Senator GARDNER. Could you give me an example of that?

Ambassador POWER. The work that Iran does to try to ensure that the U.N. Security Council does not even discuss ballistic missile launches, I assure you, is a testament to actually the stigma that they still associate with our bringing these issues before the Security Council, the same with the panel of experts actually discussing this and documenting any violation.

This is something that Iran, which, of course, wants to become a nation like any other nation within the U.N., they find it very frustrating that they continue to be scrutinized. They have never recognized, as you know, the U.N. Security Council resolutions, so the fact that the council keeps functioning, keeps oversight, keeps the spotlight on, increases the political cost, is an important step.

Senator GARDNER. In October, many members of this committee sent a letter to the Secretary of State talking about Iran's October 10 ballistic missile. The letter talks about a range of unilateral, multilateral tools available to counter Iran's missile-related activities on past occasions, imposed penalties under domestic authorities on foreign persons and entities engaged in proliferation activities.

But we have done nothing. We have imposed no penalties under domestic authorities or on foreign persons and entities, as a result of these two launches. Is that correct?

Ambassador POWER. I want to just underscore the importance of the broader ballistic missile defense efforts that we make. I feel like I have answered the question you have just posed several times, so let me try a different broadening approach, which is our response to Iranian ballistic missile launches is also a defense response. It is also the Proliferation Security Initiative. It is everything that has come out of Camp David and our engagement with the Gulf countries to ensure interoperability. It is the Iron Dome and all of the other bilateral defense arrangements that we have with the country of Israel, many of which are getting deepened, as you know, in consultations.

Senator GARDNER. They have launched twice. Is that working? If they have had two launches now, one in October, one recently, is it——

Ambassador POWER. I mean, if one is thinking in terms of regional defense, one has to take measures in order to try to ensure that our partners in the region have the tools to defend themselves.

Even if you had a designation against someone involved in the ballistic missiles program, the number one deterrent and preventive measure is going to be regional defense. That is where our emphasis was.

If I were here and we had designated another actor bilaterally— let us say we find one that has not already been designated and designate, I do not think that that would address your concern about Iran's ballistic missile program, nor should it.

So again, Iran has systematically ignored U.N. Security Council resolutions over the life of the entire international Security Council regime. The sanctions themselves were so crippling and brought us to the place where we could secure this deal because the other countries in the international system would be sanctioned if they were engaging with Iran in prohibited behavior.

Senator GARDNER. This systematic ignoring of the resolutions, does that not give you concern about their willingness to comply, going forward?

Ambassador POWER. That is why we have snapback. That is why we have verification monitoring on the ground. As the President said from the beginning, this is not an agreement predicated on trust, particularly in light of Iran's past behavior, past behavior, again, confirmed by the IAEA PMD report.

Senator GARDNER. Thank you, Mr. Chairman.

The CHAIRMAN. Before going on to Senator Kaine, I just want to reiterate, I think what Ben and I did the other day with you and the other members. I think regardless of how people may have voted on the Iran agreement, we understand that it is what is governing our actions right now with Iran. And I think on both sides of the aisle, regardless of how people voted, we want to make sure the agreement is implemented in the way that it was laid out.

And I think there has been a concern on both sides of the aisle that there is an air of permissiveness that is developing that will cause the likelihood of any pushback on Iranian violations over time to become less real. And I think that is what he's getting at and I think what people on both sides of aisle have been concerned about.

U.N. Security Council Resolution 1929 says they shall not undertake any ballistic activity. Unfortunately, JPOA says "is called upon." I do not know whether Iran views that as permissive language.

But this is an issue that I think many people on both sides of the aisle are concerned about. I cannot speak for everyone.

And what we are seeing is, again, not very vigilant steps being taken, and it is setting a precedent for the future.

With that, Senator Kaine.

Senator KAINE. Thank you, Mr. Chair.

And thank you, Ambassador Power.

You gave an interview to the PBS NewsHour on December 4, and you noted that more progress needs to be made in uniting the anti-ISIL coalition. Would our unified resolve against ISIL be clearer to our allies, to our troops, and to ISIL if Congress was willing to finally debate and vote on this matter after 16 months of war?

Ambassador POWER. Yes, Senator. Thank you for your leadership on this issue from the very start.

I think people are puzzled as to why—people that I work with, I should say, day-to-day up at the U.N.—are puzzled, given the priority that the American people and, on a bipartisan basis, both houses of Congress attach to the anti-ISIL struggle and all of the attention to it that has come over the course of the last 2 years as to how we cannot arrive at some consensus in order to be able to enshrine in legislation that which we say is true, which is, again, that this has the bipartisan backing of the American people and of the Congress.

So I think it would be a really important signal if we could get that AUMF done.

Senator KAINE. I have not done the research on this, but just from headlines and my memory, it strikes me that at least three of the U.N. Security Council nations—Britain, France, and, I am sad to say, Russia—have had their legislative bodies vote to confirm and approve after a debate their military activity against terrorism in Syria and Iraq. Is that correct?

Ambassador POWER. That is my understanding, as well, and I think other countries who are part of the coalition, but not on the Security Council, also, we could add to that list.

Senator KAINE. Germany, for example.

Ambassador POWER. Denmark, et cetera.

Senator KAINE. Bundestag acted last week.

Ambassador POWER. Yes.

Senator MARKEY. Last week, the chairman of the Senate Armed Services Committee, Senator McCain, said this, he did not say this approvingly, so I do not want to suggest that he was saying it approvingly, but when he was asked when an authorization vote would occur in Congress, he said, "It may require an attack on the United States of America."

In terms of you being able to do your job well, would it be a good idea for Congress to wait that long?

Ambassador POWER. No, it would not be a good idea for Congress to wait that long. I think this should be one issue that everyone in this country can agree upon, even those who have differences over tactics, over the number of trainers, or different aspects of the operations as they are unfolding. Everyone should agree that defeating and degrading ISIL and showing the world that this is something that is backed by the Congress, rendering these operations sustainable and enduring over what is a long struggle, would just be invaluable.

Senator KAINE. The President started this war against ISIL on August 8, which was 16 months ago yesterday. A year ago Friday, the only vote that has happened in Congress, in terms of an authorization, occurred in this committee on December 11, 2014, an authorization that was reported to the Senate floor where no action was taken on it.

The RAND Corporation issued a report to the Pentagon this week that said relying upon the 2001 and 2002 authorizations at a minimum involved legal gymnastics that were not helpful, and urged Congress to take action. It is just my hope that we will do that, and it is my hope that it will not take a kind of cataclysm that was suggested, again, disapprovingly by Senator McCain. I think Senator McCain views it the way that I do, that he thinks Congress should act.

Let me ask you this, moving to peacekeeping, a good news story, you talked about European nations having scaled back peacekeeping operations. A good news story for this committee and for this Congress is Colombia stepping up in September and saying they wanted to devote 5,000 troops to the U.N. peacekeeping mission. Colombia is also a peacekeeping participant in the multinational force and observers in the Sinai, as of relatively recently.

We sometimes wonder whether U.S. engagement on a diplomatic way can make a difference. Colombia is an example of failed state to international security partner in a way that I think this committee in a bipartisan way can be proud. And, also, three administrations, the Clinton administration, the Bush administration, and the Obama administration, have had a dedication to that.

Talk about nations like Colombia who are coming into providing peacekeeping forces for the first time and the degree to which we can encourage them.

Ambassador POWER. Thank you, Senator.

We view that commitment in very much the same way. It seemed also a real reflection of, however difficult the peace process is, and there is a lot of work left to do, but their confidence they are going to get where they need to get to be in a position to free up resources to be part of international peace and security.

Latin America has a huge contribution to make. One of the significant features of the President's summit was a number of Latin American countries announcing that they were prepared to do peacekeeping out of hemisphere, because a lot of Latin American countries had been dedicating their forces in Haiti.

I want to particularly commend Uruguay, because they have actually been taking lead within the region at mobilizing different contributions, working with the Colombians, saying this is how it worked for us, this is how it will work for you.

I also want to commend Mexico, which I visited recently, which has announced that it will break new ground and be involved in peacekeeping for the first time. It is in the midst of discussions now with the U.N. as to what form that will take.

If I could just touch upon, because I think it is such an important point, the larger point, the pulling up from Latin America, which is the dividend for us when a country makes progress domestically, whether in terms of democratization or in terms of conflict resolution.

I just am back from Sri Lanka, a place that, in the wake of its defeat of the LTTE, the people who, in effect, coined the suicide bomb, really regressed in terms of creeping authoritarianism, horrible atrocities carried out at the tail end of the war and no accountability for that.

Now there has been a change in government. Not only do we see them domestically taking on issues of accountability, trying to work on reconciliation with the Tamil population, but we also see their behavior within international institutions transformed, also making a very substantial commitment to peacekeeping, the stand they take on human rights resolutions, on Syria, on North Korea, et cetera, shifting.

So I want to just dwell on this point because sometimes one looks at the U.N. and it is just this black box where we are not getting the returns that we want, we are not getting the votes that we want. The way the U.N. changes over time is countries that comprise it change, and they become more at peace within themselves. They democratize. Their institutions get stronger. And we see a payoff, again, in terms of the critical mass of countries then that we have as partners in New York to work with.

Right now, it is still the case, though, that more than half the countries in the U.N. are not democratic. That affects the extent to which the U.N. is going to be a tool on democracy promotion or human rights enforcement, et cetera.

Senator KAINE. Thank you.

Ambassador POWER. Thank you, sir.

The CHAIRMAN. Thank you. The vote has gone off, and Senator Isakson is next. After him is Senator Menendez.

I would ask you, if you would, to chair the meeting while you are asking questions.

Senator ISAKSON. I am going to be very brief, because I have to go to the floor, too.

The CHAIRMAN. Okay, then Senator Murphy is next after Senator Menendez. If we would just keep it going, and I am going to bolt and come back. And thank you both very much. I know it will be orderly, regardless.

Senator ISAKSON. So you want me to yield to Senator Murphy after I finish?

The CHAIRMAN. If Menendez is not back. Thank you.

Senator ISAKSON. [Presiding] Thank you, Mr. Chairman, and thank you for calling this hearing. I am going to be very brief, because I have to do a part of this in just a minute on the floor.

But required reading of every Member of Congress and of every Ambassador to the United Nations ought to be Samantha Power's book "A Problem from U.N. ." If that book had been read, a lot of the problems we are talking about today in peacekeeping missions and rape being used as a military tactic and things like that, we would be a lot further along than we are today. That is a great book and everybody should read it.

Senator Corker and I went to Rwanda. We know about the Kigali Principles, and that is my first question to you.

As a country, have we adopted the Kigali Principles? Has the United States of America done that?

Ambassador POWER. As you know, we are not a substantial contributor to peacekeeping. So these principals so far have been embraced by the big countries that are putting thousands of troops in harm's way. We have 40 police officer and 40 military officers, all of whom we are incredibly grateful for.

So we have not yet, but more for that reason than any substantive objection. If you support our joining, I can convey that back.

Senator ISAKSON. Let me make my point. When I read your speech last night, you did not include this part in the speech, but it is in the printed speech, you talked the Kigali Principles and what they were developed from, which was a learning lesson, I think, from what you pointed out in "A Problem from U.N. ," your book.

The Kigali Principles, as I understand it, is that peacekeepers, their countries need to affirm that their troops will have the authorization to use force when necessary and do not have to radio back to headquarters to get approval. Is that correct?

Ambassador POWER. Correct, sir.

Senator ISAKSON. That is our problem in the Middle East right now, in terms of the United States. I do not think we have enough of that type of authorization for the rules of engagement of our own troops. I commend you for raising it on this question. But I think it is a bigger question, in terms of our being able to be effective, and that is to have the troops in the field that you have deployed, either for peacekeeping or for war, if you are at war, to have the actual authority for use of force they need to carry out their mission.

It kind of struck me that we were congratulating Sri Lanka and Korea and a lot of people who provide peacekeeping troops. Yet we as a country have very limited rules of engagement authorization right now as a practice in our own country. So that is my reason for bringing the point up.

Ambassador POWER. If I may just respond briefly, Senator, while you are here. You know, my impression is not that. I think that what President Obama has conveyed to the Secretary of Defense and to the chairman and to his commander, General Austin and the commanders on the ground, is a desire to offer strategic guidance, discuss any big shifts in the strategy at a senior level to make sure everybody is on the same page.

But there is a huge amount of tactical and operational flexibility that these commanders have. And I think you have seen, certainly, the President say publically what he has also conveyed many times privately in the Situation Room, which is, if there are ideas for how we can pursue this campaign more expeditiously in ways that increase the security dividend for the American people sooner, I want to see those ideas.

And so I am in these meetings where we are discussing the way ahead in our anti-ISIL strategy, and I, again, have not heard the commanders not getting the flexibility that they seek.

Senator ISAKSON. Thank you for your answer, and thank you for your service.

My last question is not a question but a statement, and that is to thank you. Your wagon is loaded and gets a new load every day, and I think you are doing a terrific job. But I would underscore, as I leave, Senator Cardin's remarks, and those of Senator Perdue and the chairman, the more transparency, the better for the U.N. There is a lot of suspicion, a lot of misunderstandings. And there is a lot of lack of trust out there in the general public. The more transparency we can have, particularly on who is paying what and how they are paying their share, would be helpful to the U.N. mission in having the support it really needs to carry out its intent from the beginning.

Ambassador POWER. Well, Senator, that gives me the chance to invite you to New York so you can get immersed in those budget numbers firsthand. But we would really welcome visits by members of this body, and we would give you a good and deep tour of the U.N. and so many of the Africa-related issues that you have worked so hard on.

As you know, the U.N. is on the frontlines.

Senator ISAKSON. Invitation accepted.

Ambassador POWER. Okay, great. Thank you.

Senator ISAKSON. Senator Murphy?

Senator MURPHY. Thank you, Senator Isakson.

Good morning, Ambassador Power.

The evening of the President's Sunday night speech, there was a series of social media postings by a really wonderful reporter from the New York Times, Rukmini Callimachi. She wrote a piece based on those observations the next day and the title was "U.S. Strategy Seeks to Avoid ISIS Prophecy." And the idea is that, if you really understand the fundamentals, the building blocks, of the religious perversion of ISIS, it is built upon a prophecy, a hope, a belief, that ultimately they are going to be in a military contest on the ground with the United States and with Western powers. I suspect that that acknowledgement is part of what made the President in that speech talk about not only the things we should do but the things we shouldn't do.

I understand that we are not going to be putting U.N. peace-keepers on the ground inside a complicated, violent civil war any time soon, but from a broader perspective, can you talk about, as we try to confront organizations that are in countries like Mali that have peacekeeping forces, that are trying to goad the West and, in particular, the United States into a military confrontation, why multinational and multiethnic forces are going to be perhaps best positioned, much better positioned than a majority U.S. force, to try to preserve peace and order? And maybe as part of that answer, talk about the contributions that majority-Muslim nations make to peacekeeping or could or should make in the future, if that is amongst the reasons why we should be paying more attention to investment in peacekeeping.

Ambassador POWER. Thank you, Senator Murphy. It is a complex question and set of ideas within it.

I think a key to effective deployments is legitimacy. And one of the things that multinational deployments can offer, but can also forfeit, as we have been talking about in the context of sexual abuse, is a perception of legitimacy, a perception that the whole world is behind a peacekeeping mission.

In truth, I think have a 65-nation coalition also enhances legitimacy. And the fact that countries from the region are part of that against ISIL is very important. It was something that was very important to the President to secure that kind of regional support.

The one thing that I would note in areas where terrorists are active, and Mali now with 44 deaths of peacekeepers just over the life of a mission that has been in place only a few years underscores, is that there can be a mismatch between U.N. peacekeeping and even robust U.N. peacekeeping, which we support, and the Kigali Principles show that a lot of other troop-contributing countries support, and these kinds of environments where extremists and terrorists, yes, they may make the United States their number one target, if they have that opportunity, but if there are no Americans around, they are also perfectly prepared to target Chadians and Dutch peacekeepers and Burkina Faso peacekeepers.

So I want to stress that I agree very much, I think, with the logic of the article that you have described and found it a very powerful look at ISIL's ideology.

I will use the question as an occasion to alert the committee to the extent to which peacekeeping is being increasingly seen as a soft target for terrorists and extremists in those environments that they inhabit. And we have a really significant national interest in hardening these missions, in ensuring that they have the training they need to operate in these evermore not only complex environments because conflict is still going on, but complex because you combine conflict and the actual fact that the peacekeepers themselves are a target.

And just to give you one example of how I think the Defense Department has been responsive in this regard, we are now doing more and more counter-IED training for peacekeepers. I mean, talk about not your mother's peacekeeping. If anybody would have imagined at the outset of peacekeeping that people would have to train against IEDs that were presumably targeting the peacekeepers themselves, I am not sure peacekeeping would have ever gotten off the ground.

So I think your larger point is right. Having countries who know the language, I think that is a critical component, that have cultural overlap with those countries in which they are operating is really important.

The only other challenge is that sometimes countries can be too familiar with a country. One of the reasons the international community went to U.N. peacekeeping in the first place is to try to inject actually more distance so there would be a greater perception of independence and one would not be seen as being a stakeholder on one side or the other.

So all of these factors, I think, need to be taken into account.

Senator MURPHY. [Presiding] Well, thank you. And let me add my thanks to Senator Isakson for the number of heavy lifts that you undertake for us every day in New York. Thank you for your time.

And I will turn it over to Senator Menendez.

Ambassador POWER. Thank you, Senator.

Senator MENENDEZ. Thank you.

And in appreciation of the chairman's courtesies, I am not going to ask for unanimous consent for anything I want right now, since I am here alone. [Laughter.]

Senator MENENDEZ. So let me let me, first of all, Ambassador, say I appreciate your service to our country, and I have a high regard for you.

And my own personal view is that, left to your own devices, on some issues, you might be more forward-leaning. You do not need to respond to that. It is just my observation.

Having said that, however, let me enlarge this conversation about peacekeeping. I know some of my colleagues have broached this subject already.

Peacekeeping is, yes, very important in the sense of what the core of this hearing is about, but part of the way in which you keep the peace is to make sure that the will of the international community is observed and that it is not violated, and if it is violated, that there are consequences so that, hopefully, a continuation of that breach does not lead to the outbreak of war and, therefore, what flows from that.

So I want to come to the issue of Iran. I know several of my colleagues have pursued the core of the missile test. But first of all, I would like to ask you, would you agree with me that for well over a decade, Iran, as you have said in response to some of my colleagues' questions, did not recognize U.N. Security Council resolutions and moved their nuclear program forward to a point in which it got so big—too-big-to-fail, in the bank context? Well, this was too big to actually end.

So they violated the international will purposely, and in doing so were able to get to a point that they largely wanted to. Would that be a fair observation?

Ambassador POWER. Yes, they violated international resolutions and built up their program. Again, I think this is probably not the venue to get into the extent of the program.

Senator MENENDEZ. No.

Ambassador POWER. But such that——

Senator MENENDEZ. That is pretty well-documented.

Ambassador POWER. Yes.

Senator MENENDEZ. But in any event, and in plenty of public discourse, as well.

But the point is they violated international resolutions for——

Ambassador POWER. Absolutely.

Senator MENENDEZ.—the better part of a decade.

Ambassador POWER. Yes.

Senator MENENDEZ. And during those violations, they progressed, for a good period of time without the type of sanctions regime that was largely generated by the Congress, not by the executive branch.

And so I look at that, and I look at your acknowledgement that they have not recognized Security Council resolutions, and I say to myself, there is a history here and a pattern. If you go visit the Archives building with me, over its mantel it says, "What is past is prologue."

And I have a real concern that what we have here is a lack of will by the United States and as a leader in this regard by our partners in going ahead and making sure that Iran understands that you cannot violate the international will without consequence, which I consider, even as I did not support the agreement, that to the extent that the agreement is going to produce any benefits, Iran must clearly understand that there will be consequences for not following that agreement.

And the message it seems to me that we are sending and that we have sent as a country in various iterations is quite the contrary.

So we, basically, have no real action. I heard your responses about referring it to the committee and having discussions. I get the U.N. process. But the bottom line is there have been no real actions, no consequence.

Now they have a second test, and we are talking about verifying. But at the end of the day, it took place and there will be no real consequence.

We would like to see the Security Council be the venue for a multilateral consequence, but we hear nothing in the interim about an individual consequence.

We see a set of circumstances in which I predicted as well as a whole host of others that on the question of Parchin, we were going to basically sweep this under the rug and ultimately dismiss it, which is now the resolution that is presently being circulated at the IAEA to close this chapter, because we want something bad enough we are willing to go ahead and overlook. In doing so, I think we make a grave mistake.

We did that with Cuba, because we wanted to create relations with Cuba even though they violated Security Council resolutions and shipped missiles and MiGs under tons of sugar to North Korea. Nothing happened to them.

So when we want something bad enough—when I say "we," the administration wants something bad enough—they are willing to overlook. And that is a dangerous proposition, a dangerous proposition.

So what is it that we are going to do to send a real, clear, un-equivocal, unambiguous message to the Iranians, because we were all assured here that notwithstanding the nuclear portfolio, that we could be robustly active and take actions on nonnuclear issues. Well, this is a nonnuclear issue. And conversation is not an action.

Ambassador POWER. Thank you, Senator.

So let me use this also as an occasion, since Senator Corker is back, to address a comment he made earlier, which is in keeping with what you are saying, which is his impression of a kind of greater permissiveness and your statement that somehow if you want it bad enough, you are willing to overlook, et cetera.

The way that this administration and our predecessors responded in New York to prior recurrent, as it happens over the life of the regime, violations of U.N. Security Council resolutions has not changed. There is no difference in the way that we go through this procedure, what we seek to do in New York at the U.N. Security Council. And, frankly, there is not even much difference in terms of the kinds of resistance we face from predictable quarters.

The Security Council regime, as you well know, built out and force multiplied on the sanctions that Congress put in place. And it is that regime that caused Iran to make a series of concessions that for I think the three of you here were not deemed satisfactory, but went well beyond what would have been achievable without the sanctions regime, and gives us the confidence, again, that this is a good deal and one that will dismantle Iran's nuclear weapons program.

The objective we have——

Senator MENENDEZ. With all due respect, I am not talking about the deal anymore. We are past that.

Ambassador POWER. No, we are talking about implementation of the deal.

Senator MENENDEZ. I am talking about making sure that we have enforcement of Security Council resolutions that are meaningful.

Ambassador POWER. Agreed. Agreed.

But, again, sort of the accusation is that we are seeing things differently than you, because we have a vested interest in seeing this deal implemented. We have a collective, as I think all of you agree, vested interest in seeing this deal implemented, because we do not want Iran to ever obtain a nuclear weapon. That is our objective.

And we have put in place measures. It is the expanded verification and monitoring, and even the PMD. For all of the dissatisfaction that has been expressed about the report and our approach to it, fundamentally, the IAEA was able to get access to Parchin in a way that it had not been able to in the past.

The snapback of the sanctions regime is an incredibly important tool in our arsenal, and it is leverage. Senator Corker said the other day to the Security Council that we will have given up all our leverage on the frontend. That is just not true. We will have that hanging over implementation, reporting of violations, going forward. And we will have in our toolbox the bilateral sanctions measures as a way of responding to lesser incidents of noncompliance and lesser violations.

So, again, the U.N. Security Council is one venue, and we will do as we have been doing for a decade, which is call a spade a spade, bring forward violations, increase the political cost, ensure that Iran is isolated for its violations of 1929 now and 2231, once the implementation day progresses.

But we also have a set of other tools aimed at getting at Iranian bad behavior, including ones on this body.

Senator MENENDEZ. Mr. Chairman, if I may, since my time has expired, let me just make a comment.

You know, I appreciate your answer. You are very good at answering, but not answering.

So let me just say that you talk about snapback, those sanctions that you admit and the administration has increasingly admitted brought Iran to the table, they expire this coming year. And you all negotiated away, at least as I read the agreement, the ability for the administration to support a reauthorization of it, which I intend push for, because the snapback means nothing if cannot snap back to something that is meaningful. And the administration just will not talk about that reauthorization, because, as I read the agreement, they do not have the wherewithal to agree to a reauthorization. They gave it away.

And then the last point, another example, enforcing Resolution 1701, the transfer of arms to Hezbollah. During the review of Iran nuclear agreement and defending the lifting of the U.N. arms embargo, the administration repeatedly emphasized that U.N. Security Council Resolution 1701 remains in place, and that prevents the transfer of weapons to Hezbollah, and we are going to make sure that that is the case.

Well, since the announcement of the JCPOA, Hezbollah has continued to receive arms from outside of Lebanon. So what steps have UNIFIL taken to stop the transfer of arms to Hezbollah? What steps have we taken to stop those transfers?

Ambassador POWER. Thank you, Senator. I addressed this question earlier for Senator Perdue, but it is a very important question.

I think the point that was made over the course of the discussion about the JCPOA is that authorities, that this body and we were understandably concerned, were going away or could go away at some point under the JCPOA. Many of those authorities were elsewhere in other Security Council resolutions. So I think that was the implication of 1701, in that context.

Look, as I said earlier, Hezbollah is a terrorist organization, and UNIFIL is a peacekeeping mission. UNIFIL's job is to do everything in its power to deter Hezbollah from amassing weapons, to call a spade a spade, and to call them out when they are, to alert us and other stakeholders to anything that comes to their attention that, again, is alarming in this regard.

As you know, over the life of UNIFIL, I think it has had a constructive effect on events on the ground. I do not think the Government of Israel would support its perpetuation if it had not. But is it a panacea for Hezbollah? No, it is not. And, no, it will not be.

I think that we have really pressed the U.N. to step up its reporting and to sound the alarm and to shine the spotlight and to do the things that it can do. But in terms of armed confrontation with Hezbollah, that is not something UNIFIL is perusing.

We are also trying to enhance the capabilities of troops who comprise UNIFIL, which is one of the stronger missions, because of the European presence. And we are hopeful, again, that the peacekeeping summit that the President chaired will give us a broader pool of troops to draw from, so as to make sure that that mission is right-sized.

Senator MENENDEZ. Well, thank you, Mr. Chairman. I would just say that no consequences is a green light to violations. And that is what I see us doing.

The CHAIRMAN. [Presiding] Thank you.

Before I turn to Senator Markey, while Senator Menendez is here, it is true that it is highly unlikely that the U.N. Security Council will take any actions relative to the violations of UNSCR 1929. Is that correct?

Ambassador POWER. Again, we have already taken action.

The CHAIRMAN. The answer is yes.

Ambassador POWER. We have already taken action.

The CHAIRMAN. But——

Ambassador POWER. We have brought the issue to the Council. This is what we did——

The CHAIRMAN. But I am talking about as far as sanctions, penalties.

Ambassador POWER. I would not assess that——

The CHAIRMAN. It is not likely that Russia or China will go along with——

Ambassador POWER. I share your assessment on Russia and China.

The CHAIRMAN. Okay, so let me just say this.

Ambassador POWER. Yes.

The CHAIRMAN. When you say that it is untrue what I said, relative to——

Ambassador POWER. That the administration was being more permissive in terms of sanctions violations. That was what I heard you say.

The CHAIRMAN. Well, we will see. Nothing has happened yet.

What I said was that the leverage shifts to Iran. They are at breakneck speed dismantling so that they get the sanctions relief they are after, which we would expect. Now people believe that in January or February, they will get all of the sanctions relief they are after.

And for you to say that snapback is a real tool when it is contingent upon the countries that are participating implementing back those sanctions, and we have countries like Russia and China, which probably, likely, we know, are not going to push back against this issue.

If there are incremental violations, all of the leverage is with Iran. That is a fact. It is not incorrect. It is with Iran because there is no way that this administration is going to consider challenging an incremental violation because they know all Iran has to do is step out. And they know that Russia and China and, candidly, probably our Western friends in Europe are not really going to force them to comply.

So it is a true statement, not an untrue statement, that the leverage ends up with Iran because they have what they want. We have given it up, and we have partners at the U.N. Security Council that are not going to cooperate with us.

Senator Markey?

Senator CARDIN. Let me just interject for one second. I apologize to Senator Markey.

I think a lot of us share that frustration. I would just urge us to work with our European allies on the timing of a response to the violation of the ballistic missiles.

We all share the frustration that there is unlikely to be sanction action by the Security Council, but if we demonstrate action with our European partners, particularly in the P5, I think it would be a signal to Iran that these types of activities are not going to go unchallenged.

Ambassador POWER. Senator Markey, would you mind if I just respond very briefly? I am so sorry.

But I want to underscore that when we went to the council once we confirmed the violation on October 10, we did so with the United Kingdom, with France, and with Germany. And I think doing something like that irrespective of what further tangible outcome we were able to secure from the council is going to be very important in perhaps even broadening that.

Mr. Chairman, the one thing I feel compelled to say is that when you say they are going with breakneck speed to dismantle, it is very important to remember that that is a good thing. That is what we want, that breakneck speed, the dismantlement.

So understanding again that there is pay for performance as part of the deal, that is the way that we have incentivized them moving forward and allowing the inspectors in.

But sometimes in the way that this is discussed, you would think that that is not a good thing. That is a good thing. That is the point of the deal, to get them to dismantle their program.

The CHAIRMAN. No, I understand that. I understand they are dismantling antique centrifuges, and we are allowing them to continue development of IR–2s, IR–4s, IR–6s, IR–8s. I understand that.

And look, again, I do not want to re-debate the agreement. What I think we are focused on right now is that the international community knows that they violated UNSCR 1929, and in essence, they are violating the spirit of JPOA, where they are called upon not to do this. And we all know that the U.N. Security Council is not going to take action.

That is what is important to us, because we believe that after they get the sanctions relief, after they dismantle these antiques that they are using right now, these IR–1s, that they are going to push the envelope.

And we believe that you and others there, by not taking even bilateral action yet, are helping create an air of permissiveness.

Even though we like you and respect you, we have a policy difference here. This is not directed at you. It is directed at the U.N. Security Council.

Senator Markey?

Senator MARKEY. Thank you, Mr. Chairman, very much.

Thank you for all your great work, Ambassador. I know it is global and complex, but you just serve our country so well. Thank you.

Could we come back, if we could for a second, to Syria? When I look at Assad, when I look at all of his supporters inside of the country, he has upwards of 30 percent of the army as Sunni soldiers who will not be viewed well when there is a peace agreement by the other Sunni soldiers that have been trying to depose Assad for all these years—similarly, the Alawite soldiers who are fighting for him.

So they will be looking for protection, if there is a peace agreement. And I think Secretary Kerry and his entire team are doing a great job in moving us toward that. But there will have to be protection for these people to avoid—and I think they would be foolish not to anticipate this—what happened in Iraq, what happened in Libya, what happened in Egypt.

So they are going to be looking for protection, and that kind of looks to the U.N. It looks to these blue-helmeted soldiers to come in and to give some level of guarantee that there will protection for them if they lay down their guns.

Otherwise, I do not see a resolution of it. I just see a protracted war where no matter how hard you try to negotiate a peaceful settlement, you just wind up with an ever-continuing conflict.

So could you talk about that a little bit and what role U.N. peacekeepers could play in a post-peace agreement, understanding that we are far from that, but just looking at, anticipating, a potential role for the U.N. or some other multinational force to move in and to give some guarantees?

Otherwise, I do not think Assad is ever leaving. You just look at it from a perspective of human nature and looking at what has happened in all these other countries, they will be dead. They will be killed. I mean, the revenge motivation is just going to be so high, given the tragedy that has affected these other families. And then we have yet another cycle that we have participated in.

So how could the U.N. or another multinational force play a constructive role?

Ambassador POWER. Well, there is no shortage of very complex dimensions to imagining a political settlement for Syria. But you put your finger on I think one the hardest issues of all, which would be any notional reintegration of Syrian moderate opposition forces with Syrian Government troops, whether the air force, which have been involved in barrel-bombing and chemical weapons use, or the infantry. I mean, it is going to be extremely difficult. And as you say, we are not at this point of the discussions.

But in order for there to be an agreement on a political transition by mutual consent, which is the catchphrase from Geneva and is the operative principle for Vienna, that is going to be one of the questions that both sides are asking, because it cuts in the other direction as well. When moderate opposition forces go back to their home communities from which they have been purged, what happens to them if the forces in control remain, in large, government forces?

So where that confidence-building comes from, who the guarantors are of any kind of reintegration—and this gets back to Senator Cardin's question earlier—what the accountability mechanism is whereby there can be some healing or truth telling and punishment for those who committed the worst violations, all of those modalities have to be worked through.

Senator MARKEY. On both sides.

Ambassador POWER. On both sides, again, yes, absolutely.

Now in terms of the near term, we have ISIL with a very extensive presence in Syria that is shrinking but nonetheless would be a significant consideration for any outside country thinking about deploying troops to Syria. We have al Qaeda's affiliate al-Nusra as well. Part of what is being worked through in Vienna, as you know, are definitions of who is a terrorist and who is not, so that there can be, at a strategic level at least, an idea that everybody can go against these forces together.

But I think what you would need, if one was going with a troop presence from the outside, would you would have to make a judgment that a troop presence would do more good than harm, that it would invite and create more confidence. To have that confidence, those Alawites and Sunni soldiers on the government side and then Sunni moderates on the other side are going to have to believe that those troops are going to protect them, if they get attacked.

If you look at U.N. peacekeeping missions as the first part of the hearing, that is not always the case around the world, right? Some troop contributors, that is not a role they play eagerly, even if that is part of the mandate.

So then you could look at a regional force or a green-hatted force of some kind. You would still ask that question: Are troop contributors ready to invest themselves in enforcing this agreement? Is that something that some of our allies would be a part of?

And the only caution I would give in terms of a regional force, which is something I think that is being looked at—again, all the costs and benefits of all of these permutations have to be thought through. On the one hand, you would have the language. You would have the cultural affinities. But in the case of many of the regional players, they have been stakeholders in this conflict, so the idea is that they would then be seen as impartial.

So finding a confidence-building mechanism that does not run afoul of being seen to be a party to the conflict, and where they would be willing to put their troops in harm's way on behalf of this agreement, is going to be one of the challenges we have to think through if the parties deem an outside force a necessary part of this political agreement.

Senator MARKEY. I do not see how you can avoid it. I just think that the recrimination coefficient is going to be historically high. The carnage has just been so great on both sides. And the bitterness, the acrimony will not settle out for decades. And we need some mechanism as an intervention that allows for a period of reconciliation, of healing.

And I think in the absence of a very well thought out plan that is put together, and I think it should be put together sooner rather than later just a concept that could move in to assuage the concerns that all parties are going to have, that the removal of Assad does not ultimately lead to a repetition syndrome breaking out inside of the country in yet a different cycle that seeks to extract a revenge against those with whom they have grievances.

So I just think the sooner we kind of think that through and what we are going to put in there, I think the better the conversations that we can have to give some assurances to the more responsible parties who might want to end this war that the death toll is not just going to continue to mount.

So removing Assad is just one step. I think that it has to be accompanied by a set of guarantees that it is just not going to be mass carnage afterward.

But I think I feel very good knowing that you are there and Secretary Kerry is there and thinking all these issues through. Thank you so much.

The CHAIRMAN. Well, thank you for being with us. I think you can see that that we are getting close to the end here.

I do want to chase just for a moment, if I could, the conversation you had with Senator Kaine.

Do your colleagues at the United Nations think that somehow Congress and the American people do not want to defeat ISIS?

Ambassador POWER. I do not think they would have that impression. My response was that they are puzzled as to why we cannot come up with an authorization here together——

The CHAIRMAN. And are they puzzled by the fact that the administration has told us over and over and over again here at this committee—Secretary Kerry, Secretary Carter, the White House sending over notes—that they have all the authorities they need to continue the fight against terrorism that was authorized in 2001? Is that confusing to them?

Ambassador POWER. I think, again, I was not speaking——

The CHAIRMAN. That is your——

Ambassador POWER. If I may, I was not speaking to the legal authorities question. I do not think anybody questions whether or not the United States has the authority to carry out the campaign that we are carrying out.

I think the question is, as a political symbol and as reinforcement of the effort that we are making, that there should be an ability to get consensus here.

The CHAIRMAN. Well, there is consensus. I mean, the President has the authority——

Ambassador POWER. I am sorry. My response was on an AUMF, consensus on an AUMF.

The CHAIRMAN. It is a little game that is being played. It is difficult for me to understand. I mean, on one hand, witness after witness after witness comes up here and tells us they have all the authorities they need. And then people like you and others come up and talk about how it would be nice.

I guess I do not get it. I voted for an authorization in 2013. I helped craft it to go against Assad. And we turned away from that.

So certainly, this committee is willing to take up tough issues when a declaration of war is occurring.

And has the President declared war on ISIS? Has he declared war on ISIS? Has he laid out a strategy publicly to defeat ISIS?

So I just want to say, I am sorry this cutesy thing that has been occurring recently, especially over the last 2 weeks. I am having difficulty understanding when I agree with the administration.

They have every authority that they need to defeat and destroy ISIS.

So I do not know what is up. Maybe the President is receiving criticism, and he is trying to deflect that to Congress somehow. I do not know what is occurring.

But all I can say with you, I am in full agreement with the administration that the 2001 authorization, while certainly on the edges, gives them the authority to do everything they could possibly want to do to destroy ISIS. And I believe that everyone in the world, everyone in the world, understands that Congress wants to see that happen.

Ambassador POWER. Let me be clear. The President has himself, as you know, made clear that he has the authority to prosecute this campaign effectively. I was responding to Senator Kaine's comment that a number of the other countries in the coalition have gone through a domestic legislative process of——

The CHAIRMAN. They did not have the authorities to do what they were doing. They did not have the authorities. Is that correct?

Ambassador POWER. I would have to go case by case, and I am not familiar with the domestic legal machinations in these countries.

The CHAIRMAN. Well, certainly, Great Britain's or U.K.'s unwillingness——

Ambassador POWER. Yes, I think in parliamentary systems, they need to go through the exercise that they have gone through.

I think this is a reason though that the question is a little bit more in the air than it has been over the last 6 months up in New York.

The CHAIRMAN. I think it is in the air for——

Ambassador POWER. But the President has said he has the authorities he needs. There is no resurrecting or surfacing this issue for any other reason.

The CHAIRMAN. So you agree 100 percent that the President has the authority.

Ambassador POWER. Absolutely.

The CHAIRMAN. Has the President declared war on ISIS, by the way?

Ambassador POWER. I believe he has said we are going to defeat and destroy ISIS, ISIL.

The CHAIRMAN. Look, we thank you for being here today and certainly respect the job that you have. You are very bright and intelligent. Sometimes I take issue with you when I feel like you are carrying too much the administration's line. But I understand sometimes you feel compelled to do so.

I thank you for being here, and we wish you well as you take demonstrative action against UNSCR 1929 being violated over the next week or so. Thank you.

So our next panel will consist of two more outstanding witnesses. The first witness is the Honorable John Negroponte, vice chairman of McLarty and Associates and former United States Permanent Representative to the U.S. Mission to the United Nations, the same job our former witness is occupying.

Our second witness will be Dr. Bruce Jones, vice president of the Foreign Policy Program at the Brookings Institute.

Again, we thank Ambassador Power for being here. Both of you have witnessed what just happened. We hope you can summarize your thoughts in about 5 minutes. And we look forward to questions.

Again, thank you for being here.

John, why don't you start?

STATEMENT OF HON. JOHN NEGROPONTE, VICE CHAIRMAN, MCLARTY ASSOCIATES, WASHINGTON, D.C.

Ambassador NEGROPONTE. Yes, sir. Thank you, Chairman Corker, Ranking Member Cardin. It is a pleasure to appear before you this morning to discuss United Nations peacekeeping, a subject of importance to United States security.

When I was Ambassador to the United Nations, this subject was frequently on the agenda of the U.N. Security Council. During my tenure there, peacekeeping operations were stood up in Sierra Leone and Liberia, among other countries. And, of course, we also renewed a number of operations that continue to this day, such as in the Democratic Republic of Congo, the Western Sahara, and so-forth.

I want to state categorically at the outset my conviction that United States' support for U.N. peacekeeping operations is in the overwhelming national security interests of our country. There are three major reasons for, which I hold this view. I call these three arguments, first, cost; second, the boots-on-the-ground argument; and three, legitimacy. I will explain each of these thoughts further.

First, with respect to cost, the United Nations has more than 100,000 troops deployed in peacekeeping operations around the world today. The approximate cost of deploying these forces is $8 billion per year, which, of course, is a small fraction of what we spend in our own national defense budget.

Our share of these costs is less than $3 billion, a small fraction, again, and some illustrative figures were cited by Senator Cardin, a small fraction of what it would cost to deploy United States forces on similar missions.

This is not a trivial argument. In today's world and with the high cost of deploying U.S. forces to overseas missions, clearly it is an important advantage for us to know that we have considerably less expensive options available to us regarding whose forces might be available to carry out an intervention we deem to be in our interests.

Second, the boots-on-the-ground argument, this, of course, is an argument related to financial costs. Just as we benefit from the lower cost of U.N. peacekeeping budgets as compared to our own defense spending, we also do not deploy our own combat forces to these situations.

This is a huge benefit. It is hard to imagine sustained support for a hypothetical situation wherein U.S. combat units were deployed to five or 10 peacekeeping operations abroad. The costs in U.S. blood and treasure would be unacceptably high. And the spotlight on the situations in which U.S. forces were involved could undermine the kind of support and patience required in some of these very difficult situations.

So support for U.N. PKOs saves us from having to contemplate these possibilities. It also enables us to think about choices other than a stark selection between U.S. boots on the ground, on the one hand, or nothing at all.

Third, legitimacy. How many times have we undertaken or contemplated intervention without the legitimating imprimatur of a United Nations Security Council resolution?

In early 2003, I was in the well of the Security Council arguing for a Chapter VII Security Council resolution permitting the use of force against Iraq. We failed to achieve that resolution and soon thereafter intervened in Iraq with a coalition of the willing.

I am not saying that a PKO would have been appropriate at that point in time in Iraq. But what I do want to highlight is that we subsequently paid a high domestic and international price for intervening in Iraq without the support and blessing of a U.N. Security Council resolution.

By definition, a U.N. peacekeeping operation has consensus support within the P5 and the blessing of a Security Council resolution.

This is an important political and legal advantage, which should not be dismissed lightly.

Senator Corker, Ranking Member Cardin, I know there are issues regarding the effectiveness, comportment, and leadership of some PKOs, and these are issues that will require continued attention and effort from troop-contributing and other U.N. members alike. And given our leadership role in the world and our status as the U.N.'s largest single financial contributor, we have a special responsibility in this regard. But whatever imperfections or blemishes might exist in the U.N. peacekeeping setup, it is our responsibility to help address these issues in a constructive way.

With steady engagement from the U.S. and others, I foresee continued improvement in the performance and utility of PKOs and even their more creative use in addressing some of the very difficult security challenges around the globe.

Thank you for the opportunity to appear before the committee on such an important topic. I would be pleased to try to answer any questions.

[The prepared statement of Ambassador Negroponte follows:]

PREPARED STATEMENT OF HON. JOHN D. NEGROPONTE

Chairman Corker, Ranking Member Cardin, Members of the Senate Foreign Relations Committee, it is a pleasure to appear before you this morning to discuss United Nations Peacekeeping, a subject of importance to United States security.

When I was Ambassador to the United Nations, this subject was frequently on the agenda of the U.N. Security Council. During my tenure there peacekeeping operations were stood up in Sierra Leone and Liberia, among other countries and, of course, we also renewed a number of operations that continue to this day, such as in the Democratic Republic of Congo, the Western Sahara and so-forth.

I want to state categorically at the outset my conviction that United States support for U.N. peacekeeping operations is in the overwhelming national security interest of our country. There are three major reasons for which I hold this view. I call these three arguments: 1) Cost; 2) "Boots on the Ground"; and 3) Legitimacy. I will explain each of these three thoughts further. But before I do, let me mention what I consider to be the fundamental rationale for PKO's in the first place. Situations arise around the world, either because of state-to-state conflict, civil strife or state failure that require outside forces to maintain peace and order. And these forces are frequently required in substantial numbers because numbers matter when it comes to keeping the peace. Send peacekeepers in adequate numbers to deal with a situation and their presence can have a rapid calming effect. Send them in insufficient numbers and their deterrent effect can be degraded, thereby inviting trouble from those opposed to the peace we are trying to uphold. More and more, U.N. peacekeepers have been called upon to maintain the peace in situations of civil strife, especially in Africa. And protecting endangered civilians has increasingly been included in their mandates. Though the record of U.N. PKO's has been mixed, their efforts over the years have resulted in some important successes.

Let me return to the three factors I alluded to earlier: 1) First, cost: The U.N. has more than 100,000 troops deployed in PKO's around the world today. The approximate cost of deploying these forces is $8 billion per year. Our share of these costs is less than $3 billion, a small fraction of what it would cost to deploy US forces on similar missions. This not a trivial argument. In today's world and with the high cost of deploying US forces to overseas missions, clearly it is an important advantage for us to know that we have considerably less expensive options available to us regarding whose forces might be available to carry out an intervention we deem to be in our interest;

2) Second: The "Boots on the Ground" argument: This of course is an argument related to financial costs. Just as we benefit from the lower cost of U.N. peacekeeping budgets as compared to our own defense spending, we also do not deploy our own combat forces to these situations. This is a huge benefit. It is hard to imagine sustained public support for a hypothetical situation wherein US combat units were deployed to five or ten PKO's abroad. The costs in US blood and treasure would be unacceptably high and the spotlight on the situations in which US forces were involved could undermine the kind of public support and patience required in some of these very difficult situations. So, support for U.N. PKO's saves us from having to contemplate these possibilities. It also enables us to think about choices other than US boots on the ground or nothing at all;

3) Third, Legitimacy: How many times have we undertaken or contemplated intervention without the legitimating imprimatur of a U.N. Security Council Resolution? In early 2003 I was in the well of the Security Council arguing for a Chapter VII UNSC resolution permitting the use of force against Iraq. We failed to achieve that resolution and soon thereafter intervened in Iraq with a coalition of the willing. I am not saying that a PKO would have been appropriate at that point in time in Iraq. But what I do want to highlight is that we subsequently paid a high domestic and international price for intervening in Iraq without the support and blessing of a UNSC resolution. By definition, a U.N. PKO has consensus support within the P-5 and the blessing of a Security Council Resolution. This is an important political and legal advantage which should not be dismissed lightly.

Senator Corker, Ranking Member Cardin, Members of the Committee: I know there are issues regarding the effectiveness, comportment and leadership of some PKO's; and these are issues that will require continued attention and effort from troop contributing and other U.N. members alike. And given our leadership role in the world and our status as the U.N.'s largest single financial contributor, we have a special responsibility in this regard. But whatever imperfections or blemishes might exist in the U.N. Peacekeeping setup, it is our responsibility to help address these issues in a constructive way. With steady engagement from the US and others, I foresee continued improvement in the performance and utility of PKO's and even their more creative use in addressing some of the very difficult security challenges around the globe.

Thank you for the opportunity to appear before the Committee on such an important topic. I would be pleased to try to answer any questions you might have.

The CHAIRMAN. Thank you so much.

Dr. Jones?

STATEMENT OF DR. BRUCE JONES, VICE PRESIDENT AND DIRECTOR, FOREIGN POLICY PROGRAM, BROOKINGS INSTITUTION, WASHINGTON, D.C.

Dr. JONES. Thank you very much. Chairman Corker, Ranking Member Cardin, thank you for having me appear before this body, and thank you for your leadership in sustaining attention to this issue.

We have covered a lot of ground, so I will be brief and just try to reinforce a couple of points and raise a couple of additional ones.

I think this body well understands the purpose of peacekeeping is to give the United States a tool for what I have described as manning the outer perimeter, for burden-sharing in conflicts where we have an interest but we do not want to have to deploy U.S. forces or tackle the issue ourselves. I think that is well-understood in this body.

I think it is important to remember that in the majority of the cases where the U.N. is deployed, it is not deployed alone. It is often a regional organization and the U.N. co-deployed in a hybrid operation. I think we do not focus on that enough. The U.N. is an important part of the equation, but it is not the only part of the equation. And we need to sustain attention to the way that regional organizations expand the reach of the U.N. and reinforce what the U.N. can do.

That being said, of course, the U.N., as you as you both highlighted, as a burden-sharing tool, as a global burden-sharing tool, gives us the capacity to reach across the globe, to get Indian troops to work with us in Central Africa, or Brazilian troops to work with us in East Timor as they did, or European forces working with us in Haiti, that regional organizations cannot perform.

And so for all its flaws and weaknesses, the U.N. is the only genuinely global burden-sharing tool we have. And I think it is extremely important at a time when—Senator Murphy I think mentioned Colombia, but there are others like Korea and Indonesia and Brazil, rising democracies who want to do more on the international stage. The U.N. is the only tool that they have to do that.

So how do we improve the U.N.'s performance? I think of this as having four dimensions: effectiveness, efficiency, legitimacy, and leadership.

Effectiveness, I want to reinforce something that Ambassador Power said that I think is important, which is bringing countries with advanced military capabilities back into the U.N. A number of you stressed the complexity of the challenges that the U.N. confronts. I think we have to be clear eyed about the fact in a number of cases, the U.N. is operating in theaters where transnational terrorist organizations also are operating. Those are not challenges that can be met by troops with low-order capabilities.

When we look at the situation in Mali, when we look at the situation in different contexts, we are going to have to see peacekeeping have within it countries with advanced military capabilities to perform the functions of protection of civilians and implementation of mandates. So I am very supportive of the administration efforts to bring European and rising states back into peacekeeping.

An additional point that I would make, and again, Senator Murphy touched on it, is that there are different ways that the U.N. can structure its missions. We tend to focus on blue helmet operations, which are commanded by the Secretary. There is actually an alternative, which are multinational force operations, where a single member state takes the command. And that is sometimes an effective tool, because there are member states like Canada and Australia and others who have a far higher degree of capability in command and control and intelligence than the U.N. Secretary has at his disposal. That variation of using an U.N.-authorized multinational force is something I think we should be thinking about more than we sometimes do.

Quickly, on efficiency, nobody would accuse the U.N. of being an efficient organization. But it has made an important step forward with the creation of the Department of Field Support, which is a separate tool to structure and manage the U.N. field operations. The absurdity is that the politics of the General Assembly means that the Department of Field Support still has to run all of its decisions past the Department of Management, which is the headquarters tool. So the same tool that manages workshops and conferences in New York has to approve all the decisions of a more nimble tool, the Department of Field Support.

I think one of the things the United States could do is work in a coalition to change that, so that the Department of Field Support has more direct authority to oversee and implement peacekeeping operations without that kind of extra layer of a dual-key system, which is inefficient. And, of course, we have to keep working on this scale assessment issue.

Third, I would just reiterate the things that are being said on sexual exploitation. I think the U.N. makes a fundamental mistake when it does not recognize that even though this is an issue of a minority of troops and a minority of missions, it severely erodes the legitimacy of the U.N. on the ground and in capitals.

You have all said a number of things already about the United States putting the right kind of pressure on the U.N. to live up to a zero-tolerance policy, which, rather belatedly, Ban Ki-Moon came to.

And that goes to my last point, and I will end here, which is that this is also about leadership. We are coming to the end of Ban Ki-Moon's term, and I think it should be a matter of priority for the United States, when they get into the business of selecting a new Secretary General, to be paying attention to the question of whether they are focused on the effectiveness and efficiency of the U.N. in contributing to international peace and security and to work closely with the Secretary General when she or he is selected and other members of the P5 to make sure that she has available to her a deep roster of political organizational talent on which to draw in selecting top officials for the management of political peacekeeping and humanitarian operations.

I will end there.

[The prepared statement of Dr. Jones follows:]

PREPARED STATMENT OF DR. BRUCE JONES

Chairman Corker, Ranking Member Cardin, and Members of the Committee, thank you for the opportunity to address this body on the timely and consequential subject of peacekeeping and the U.S. national interest.

I'd like to start with four main points, and then suggest some key areas for reform.

First, when we address the subject of international peacekeeping, we have to start with an essential question: does the United States want to have at its disposal a tool for burden-sharing for far-flung crises, or does it want to do the job itself? That's the fundamental issue.

The right way to think about international peacekeeping is as a tool for sharing the burden of "manning the outer perimeter." We're never going to rely on international peacekeeping for core security tasks, but when we move beyond those matters of primary national security, we have three choices: do nothing, and live with the consequences—in the form of refugees, in the form of spreading instability, in the form of safe havens for terror networks; tackle these problems ourselves—even when they arise in places like the Central African Republic or northern Uganda or Yemen or northern Mali; or build and manage multilateral tools for maintaining stability and security in non-vital regions that distribute the commitment among many nations. It seems evident that the third of these is the only credible option—building tools for burden-sharing in the mission to uphold stability. The existence of such tools doesn't preclude U.S. engagement, but it gives us options.

Second, then, we have to look at the tools at our disposal, including but not limited to the U.N. It's rarely the case that the U.N. is the sole tool we are going to use to tackle a problem of civil war or humanitarian crisis. There are regional organizations, NATO, the African Union, and coalitions of the willing; as well as tools for the development of economic and governance institutions, such as the World Bank. In the vast majority of cases today, two or more of these entities are involved in producing solutions or tamping down problems. One of the weaknesses of current U.S. policy is that we treat these institutions or tools as if they are stand-alone entities; in actuality, they almost always work in concert, albeit in imperfect ways. This is all the more important given that we now confront a U.N. Security Council in which Russia is inclined to block unified action, at least in cases where it is directly involved.

Third, that being said, we should take the signal from the reality that in the vast majority of those cases, the U.N. does play an important role—in the humanitarian response; in the political response; and in the security response—all of which are supported through the peacekeeping tool. The reason the U.N. shows up in so many cases arises from a very basic but very important fact: The United Nations is a global institution, rather than a regional one, making it's tools global in scope. U.N. peacekeeping is the only mechanism we have at our disposal that allows us to combine forces from every region in the world to tackle crises or conflicts wherever they occur. Regional organizations can't produce Indian troops working with us in central Africa; or Brazilian troops working with us in East Timor, as they did; or European forces working with us in Haiti. Thus, for all its flaws and weaknesses, the U.N. is the only tool available to us for genuinely global burden-sharing. And that's all the more important at a point in time when rising democracies like Korea, Indonesia, and Brazil want to do more, not less, on the international stage, and don't have any alternatives to the U.N.

Fourth, and critically, when we hear about peacekeeping, we hear most about failures and setbacks. Even the most optimistic literature about U.N. and international peacekeeping suggests that it fails approximately 40% of the time. But that should not obscure the 60% of the time when it succeeds, or succeeds in part—either helping to end a war, securing a part of territory, or protecting a portion of a population.[1] Success is not categorized by the building, or rebuilding, of secure democracies overnight—we have to have maintain reasonable expectations of peacekeeping.

So how do we improve the ratio between success and failure? We have to work on four fronts:

- This is about effectiveness—and first and foremost that means getting better quality troops into the U.N.
- It's about efficiency, especially cost efficiency.
- It's about putting an end to sexual exploitation and abuse—actions that erode the local and international legitimacy of peacekeeping.
- And it's about leadership.

The most important issue is effectiveness—if the U.N. isn't helping to create a solution, then the question of whether its operations are efficient or legitimate is moot. The most important determinant of effectiveness is the quality of troops that participate in operations—that is to say, their capacity to undertake complex stabilization operations. When conflicts are relatively easy, i.e. when the state or the rebels in question are of low capacity, then the U.N. can draw troops from whichever nation is willing, gathering a coalition for action that can keep the lid on things. But, as we confront more resilient actors in tougher settings—especially as the geography of intra-state and proxy conflict shifts from sub-Saharan Africa to the Middle East and North Africa—we need the participation of both the European allies and the rising powers if we're going to have the capable troops needed to produce security outcomes required on the ground. This is all the more true as we

---

[1] For the comprehensive study behind these figures, see Virginia Page Fortna's 2008 book: "Does Peacekeeping Work?", specifically chapter five. See: Fortna, V. P. (2008). Does Peacekeeping Work? Princeton, NJ: Princeton University Press.

deal with the reality that in a growing portion of wars, at least one actor is engaged in terrorist activities, often with a transnational link.

I am therefore very supportive of the Obama Administration's efforts—colloquially, the Biden initiative—to bring European actors back into the fold and engage rising states in U.N. peacekeeping efforts for the provision of both troops and enabling capacities.[2]

Effectiveness also means being flexible about how we structure these forces. We tend to focus on the traditional "blue helmet" operations, that is, operations controlled centrally by the U.N. Secretariat. There's a powerful alternative in the U.N.'s toolkit, namely U.N.-mandated multi-national forces. These are operations that fly under a U.N. banner but are led and commanded by an individual state, rather than the U.N. Secretariat. Australia has led such multinational forces (in East Timor), as has Canada (in the Congo). The United States commands such a force in the Sinai (MFO Sinai). We should put more emphasis on using this option, and some of its variants.

It would be worth the effort for the United States to do a detailed examination of the range of alternatives available to the U.N.—from blue helmet operations to multi-national forces to so-called hybrid operations (where the U.N. and a regional organization fuse their forces into a single structure); such a study would enable the United States to better support and more firmly encourage the U.N. to explore a variety of options when confronted with an emerging conflict.

Then let's turn to efficiency. Nobody would accuse the U.N. of being an efficient organization. However, to be fair, during Ban Ki-Moon's term, two dynamic women, Susanna Malcorra and Ameerah Haq, effectively built the U.N.'s Department of Field Support into a more robust tool for undertaking complex field operations.

Unfortunately, the U.N.'s rules still mean that decisions made in the Department of Field Support are subject to the arcane and cumbersome tools of the Department of Management, which oversees headquarters operations. This dual key system introduces major inefficiencies and unnecessary redundancy. The United States could lead, or at a minimum offer support for, a political coalition to build on the new proposals from Ban Ki-Moon's high-level panel to increase the flexibility and efficiency of the U.N.'s field support tools.[3] This set of ideas is similar in spirit to a proposal made by former U.S. permanent representative to the United Nations Ambassador John Bolton for stand-alone management arrangements for U.N. peacekeeping.

Over time, of course, the United States will also have to secure a better arrangement for U.N. peacekeeping dues: a situation where the U.S. share of the global economy has shrunk from approximately 25% to 21%, and its share of U.N. peacekeeping dues has grown to 28%, is obviously unsustainable.[4] China has shown that it is willing to do more in voluntary funding of the U.N.'s operations, and its own rates continue to rise; but eventually this scale of assessment will have to be reworked. But the United States also has to recognize that, contra the "American decline" narrative, it is still the only global power, the only power with the capability to act in every theater, and thus the actor that most profits in real terms from burden-sharing.

The U.N. also has to address a problem that eats away at its legitimacy—sexual exploitation and abuse. No other issue so profoundly erodes the trust of local populations, or the confidence of the international community, in U.N. operations than incidences of sexual misconduct or abuse by U.N. peacekeepers. Let's be clear: this is a problem of a very small number of troops in a minority of operations. But the U.N. leadership makes a grave mistake when it doesn't recognize that it's a fundamental challenge to the legitimacy of U.N. operations. Kofi Annan eventually recognized this, and adopted a zero tolerance strategy; and, rather belatedly, Ban Ki-moon has recognized this, and has adopted a new, tougher policy.[5] The United

[2] For an overview of the Biden initiative, see: Office of the Press Secretary, The White House. (2014, September 26). Summit on U.N. Peacekeeping [Fact sheet]. Retrieved December 6, 2015, from Whitehouse.gov website: https://www.whitehouse.gov/the-press-office/2014/09/26/fact-sheet-summit-un-peacekeeping.

[3] The High-level Independent Panel on Peace Operations was convened on 31 October 2014 "to undertake a thorough review of United Nations peace operations today and the emerging needs of the future." See: "Report of the High-level Independent Panel on Peace Operations on Uniting Our Strengths for Peace: Politics, Partnership and People" [PDF]. (2015, June). Retrieved from http://www.un.org/sg/pdf/HIPPO—Report—1—June—2015.pdf.

[4] The U.N.'s figures for fiscal year 2016 have the United States contributing 28.38% of total peacekeeping dues. See: "Financing Peacekeeping." (n.d.). Retrieved December 6, 2015, from U.N.org website: http://www.un.org/en/peacekeeping/operations/financing.shtml.

[5] For a 2004 statement from Secretary General Kofi Annan, see: Annan, K. (2004, November 19). Statement by the Secretary-General on allegations of sexual exploitation and abuse in the

States should be vigilant in maintaining the necessary oversight to ensure that the Secretary-General fulfills the promise of this new policy.

Finally, this is about leadership—at headquarters, and in the field. There's no percentage in commenting here on personalities. And we're coming to the end of Ban Ki-moon's term, so soon there will be a new leadership team at the U.N. In preparation for this new window of opportunity, the United States should elevate the prioritization of the identification and the selection of a Secretary-General committed to effective and efficient U.N. contributions to international security; and we should work closely with the incoming Secretary-General and the other members of the P5 to make sure that she has available to her a deep roster of political and organizational talent from which to draw in selecting top officials for the management of political, peacekeeping, and humanitarian operations.

It has become fashionable to describe the United States as a power in decline. I disagree. The United States is the only power with political, economic, and military clout both at a global level and in every region of the world. America is the only power capable of convening states (and actors beyond states) of every stripe, of every income level, and from every region. It has an extraordinary suite of allies. The dynamism of the American private sector has been on vivid display in the energy renaissance and the economic recovery from the 2009 global financial crisis.[6] China, India, and other actors have rising capacity to be sure, and with it, spreading interests. But for now, only the United States has a global responsibility, and only the United States can build the coalitions and the multilateral instruments for global security. A peacekeeping tool that is adequately manned, resourced, and supported is an important tool in upholding that security.

Thus, only with sustained U.S. attention will it be possible to ensure that we have available to us a sufficient suite of tools for stabilization and peacekeeping, at the U.N. and beyond, to meet the American interests of supporting stability without over taxing U.S. treasure and overextending U.S. forces.

Thank you again for the opportunity to address this committee.

The CHAIRMAN. Well, thank you both. I know we got off on a lot of different topics in the last panel that were a little different than the main subject, but it is rare we have the opportunity to talk to the Ambassador.

We thank you both. We know you are both friends. And obviously, with just Ben and I here, even though this will all be part of the record, which is appreciated, this is more of a conversation.

You both have experienced the frustration of seeing peacekeeping operations where people were being abused and brutalized, and yet the caveats that existed kept peacekeepers from really being able to intervene. So we have moved in a more forward manner, which from my standpoint is welcomed as we have seen helpless people be brutalized in certain areas.

What are, though, some of the challenges that, from your perspective, we most need to think about relative to that? I mean, in essence, it is an extension in some cases of actually carrying out semi-kinetic activities, right? So what are some of the things that we as a body ought to be thinking about as we progress down that path?

Dr. JONES. Thank you very much. That is an excellent question, and I think it is extremely well-put.

It is interesting to observe. At the U.N., I think you face two challenges. One, over time, as countries with more advanced capabilities, Europeans and others, have not been participating in

U.N. Mission in the Democratic Republic of the Congo (MONUC) [Press release]. Retrieved from http://www.un.org/sg/statements/?nid=1189. For Secretary-General Ban's recent statements on sexual assault in the Central African Republic, Ban, K.-M. (2015, August 12). Opening remarks to press on the Central African Republic [Press release]. Retrieved from http://www.un.org/apps/news/infocus/sgspeeches/statments—full.asp?statID=2714#.VmTuiIv45UQ

[6] For a comprehensive account of these factors, see: Jones, B. (2014). "Still Ours to Lead: America, Rising Powers, and the Tension between Rivalry and Restraint." Washington, DC: Brookings Institution Press.

peacekeeping, the practice has sort of lowered to the capability of the troops. So the willingness to go out and undertake kinetic activities, to protect civilians, to defeat rebel forces, et cetera, has diminished, and that is a challenge.

So getting more capable troops back into peacekeeping is the first necessary step.

I think an important question is what can the United States do to stiffen their will or to ensure that they are going to have will or support. One of the things I would put on the table—by the way, I would say, I am not among those who think that the United States has to put troops into peacekeeping. I do not think that that is the correct approach. I think that the United States has unique capabilities in airlift and intelligence and other kinds of things that are more important.

I would add to it over-the-horizon extraction. If we are going to ask countries to put troops on the line and take risks, first of all, it is helpful if they are more capable troops, because they are undertaking that mission. But if we are willing to provide over-the-horizon extraction and support and defense capabilities, the risks that they are taking is lessened. So I think we can be in a stronger position in encouraging people to take those risks and to take those flights if we are willing to help them if they get stuck.

Ambassador NEGROPONTE. If I could add, first of all, I would definitely agree with Dr. Jones that capacity-building, and I think that is what he was talking about in the instance, is really one of the most important challenges, if not the most important challenge we face with respect to U.N. peacekeeping.

There was also mentioned earlier in the testimony this morning about the time it takes sometimes to mobilize some of these missions. I think the Security Council and the peacekeeping department has become more effective at that.

I would add, with respect to capacity-building, the challenge we have in ensuring that there is sort of uniform level of capacity amongst the officers that are leading these different missions around the world.

I am not aware that the U.N. has any kind of peacekeeping academy. It would seem to me, if you have military deployments in excess of 100,000 people around the world, I mean, we have an academy for each of our four uniformed services in the United States. And I wonder if some kind of training institution, where you would cycle current and potential leaders of future peacekeeping missions, whether that would not be an idea worth consideration. I mean, you would have to sit down at the drawing boards and think about how you do that, but anyway, that is one idea I would like to leave for your consideration.

The CHAIRMAN. Dr. Jones, you mentioned that you do not think it is appropriate for the U.S. to have ground troops, if you will, involved. As it relates to our NATO efforts, we obviously have everything involved, money, equipment, personnel. Again, we are the provider of security services. Unfortunately, most of the members of NATO are consumers of security services.

Here, we are the largest provider of monetary resources, and, as I understand it, we have committed 42 officers to be part of peacekeeping.

But just for the record, could you tease out why it is you said what you just said? You say we should not be involved with ground troops because?

Dr. JONES. Thank you. It comes up a lot. It has come up a lot in the last year as the administration has been pushing the Europeans and other states to do more. One of the responses has been, "Well, are you going to? Are you going to put troops in?" As I said, I think the things that only the United States can do include airlift, signals intelligence, and some of the command and control functions that you just referred to.

I would not be doctrinaire about it. I do not think there is no circumstance where the United States should put troops in. I would recall that we have actually, historically. In 1995, the United States had troops under the command of a Canadian-led multinational force in eastern Zaire. We have done it. It is not impossible to do.

But by and large, it seems to me that we are better off when other troops are willing to be on the frontlines of this. Senator Murphy talked about the notion of having multiethnic and multinational forces.

The simple reality is that the United States is going to attract attention. There are going to be a lot of people who want to fight the United States. I think we are simply raising a red flag to a bull when we put U.S. forces on the ground in a number of these situations. We are much better off performing those functions that only we can provide, as well, as I mentioned, over-the-horizon rescue and support operations, and ask others to be on the frontlines.

The CHAIRMAN. It is generally the same approach, as has been discussed by most, and that is in Syria we would like to have Arab faces on the ground more predominantly than Western faces, right? It just helps ensure that there is a more cohesive nature, if you will, relative to what is happening on the ground.

Typically, we have had a policy, have we not, that U.S. troops are not going to be commanded by people other than U.S. officers, too? Is that correct?

Dr. JONES. We have had that policy. As I said, we have occasionally violated it. U.S. forces were under Canadian command in multinational force operations in Zaire very briefly. But I think as a general rule, it is the right policy.

And more to the point, as I said, there are simply too many occasions in which participation by the United States would change the political texture of the force in ways that I think would amplify the resistance to the force rather than the opposite.

Ambassador NEGROPONTE. Whereas the enablers do not necessarily have that same kind of a profile, and yet there is no other country as capable as we are of producing these vital enablers to these missions.

The CHAIRMAN. Ambassador, you have had this role. You have been at the United Nations. Senator Cardin, which I appreciate deeply, raised the issue of just our payments. We have 22 percent of the world's gross domestic product and yet we contribute 28.5 percent of the budget here.

Our other "associates," if you will, at the United Nations obviously are not doing their part, otherwise our amount would not be 28.5 percent.

We find this same to be the case—I have referred to it now three times—at NATO. It is where we desire for things to happen, it seems more so than others, and, therefore, we end up being financially exposed more than others.

You have been in this role. Tell us from your perspective what we as a country can do to seek equilibrium and to cause other countries to play their appropriate roles.

Ambassador NEGROPONTE. Well, it is frustrating. And I think you are right, Senator, to talk about kind of the mysterious ways in which the budget is negotiated, and very often right at the end of the year just before Christmas, when everyone is in a rush to get out of there. Somehow at 3 o'clock in the morning, the U.N. budget gets agreed upon. So sometimes you get some rather anomalous situations that will arise.

But I think we just have to keep working on that. I recognize that we have not been as successful as we ought to have been in keeping the peacekeeping assessments down.

But again, in proportion to what it would cost to field other kinds of forces or our own military expenditures for our own defense establishment, we are talking about relatively small amounts of money. Therefore, I think we just need to do our best but recognize that we may not achieve everything that we hope to achieve in those negotiations.

But I am also reassured that some countries now are putting up more resources than they had before. I am glad to hear that China is going to be assessed something on the order of 10 percent for peacekeeping, which, if I recall correctly, is a significant departure from 10 or 15 years ago when their contribution was a fraction of that.

The CHAIRMAN. Senator Cardin?

Senator CARDIN. Mr. Ambassador, as you were describing the U.N. budget process, I thought you were describing the U.S. budget process. [Laughter.]

Ambassador NEGROPONTE. I do not know where they learned those lessons.

Senator CARDIN. Dr. Jones, thank you very much for your service. And you come here with a great deal of expertise on the United Nations, having worked as adviser to Secretary General.

Ambassador Negroponte, you served in that position as Ambassador, and you have served in so many other positions of foreign policy.

I want to follow up on the reform issues, and I will tell you why.

But first, let me suggest to the chairman, your suggestion on training is a very important suggestion. I serve on the Board of Visitors of the U.S. Naval Academy, and I see firsthand the availability of training at the U.S. Naval Academy for some of our allied countries. We do train at our service academies foreign students.

I think an arrangement with the United Nations in regards to their peacekeeping command may very well be a viable option to get greater capacity. And I would ask our staff to take a look at that, to see whether we can look at how our service academies could assist in this regard.

It also helps us, because having a more diversified student body at our academies prepares us for the global missions that our military command needs to be aware of.

So I thought that was a very good suggestion, and I would ask if our staffs could perhaps follow up on that and see whether that is a viable option.

But I want to talk about the scale of assessments and the how these numbers come about. But I put it in context of a Senator who strongly supports the United Nations and its mission and its budget.

But if we were to put it a U.N. reform bill on the floor of the United States Senate, the type of amendments that would be offered and the types of potential restrictions on U.S. participation in the United Nations, getting a majority vote, perhaps even a 60-vote threshold, is real. The reason for that is because of the lack of transparency in the United Nations and the illogical way that they go about their budgeting.

We talk about burden-sharing, and we recognize that it is disproportionate, that the U.S. taxpayers have been asked to take on a much stronger commitment than the developed countries, those who have the capacity to do a lot more. It is true in NATO. It is true in our coalitions. It is true in individual participation globally. And it is certainly true in the United Nations.

So I understand that we are getting a good value for our contributions to the U.N. I never doubt that. I agree with you completely. And the peacekeeping missions are critically important to the U.S.

But it seems to me that we have not been as effective as we need to in the transparency and reform within the United Nations process. And if we do not deal with it in a way that is understandable to the U.S. political system, then there could be negative consequences to the U.S. participation at the United Nations.

So it is for that reason that I cannot justify a 22 percent budget allocation and then 28.5 percent on peacekeeping, particularly in light of all the other commitments that U.S. taxpayers are making to international security issues. I would just like to get your advice as to the most effective way for this Senator and for the Congress to weigh in, in a constructive way, so that we can get the type of reforms we need in the United Nations.

Ambassador NEGROPONTE. Well, I am not as current on these issues as I was when I was serving in that position, but I was the beneficiary of Richard Holbrooke's successful negotiation with respect to the last big arrears situation. It took incredible work on his part, the kind of work that only Richard Holbrooke was capable of. It was jawboning with membership, with the secretariat, working hard with Congress, like Ms. Power, bringing the Security Council down to visit the Senate, which I think was a very, very good idea. I am sure you imparted this message to them when you met with them. Those are the right people to pass that message to.

I think it just requires an intensive diplomatic effort with these countries to try and correct that situation. I am pleased we have a 22 percent assessment for the general assessment for the U.N.

Holbrooke left that issue somewhat unresolved. If I remember correctly, it was 26-point-something-or-other, and now it has gone up a percentage point or 2 since he reached his agreement.

But I think we just have to work that one really hard. And what I would hate to see happen is that the arrears become so large that then it becomes some kind of a crisis situation with regard to whether or not we are going to continue our support, which would undermine our support for the United Nations. That is the danger that I think you are describing.

Dr. JONES. I do not have much to add. I would just add one point of context, which is sort of ironical.

We spent a lot of the last few years hearing countries talk about how the United States is in a decline, a relative decline in the United States, all this kind of stuff. I profoundly disagree with that underlying notion. The reason I mention it in this case is, when you look at the scale of assessments, it was about 30 percent in the height of the post-Cold War period. It declined to about 25 percent as we made continual progress to bring the scale of assessment in line with our share of world GDP. And it has gone back up over the last 3 years. It has gone back up to 28 percent since the global financial crisis because we have done much better in recovering from the global financial crisis than a number of our allies and partners in Europe and others.

And so it is a kind of irony of the moment that whereas people talk about U.S. decline——

Senator CARDIN. It is my understanding that the difference between 22 percent and 28 percent is not our share in the global economy. It is justified by our seat on the Security Council, which many of us interpret it is to bust the 22 percent cap.

Dr. JONES. It is both, because the formula starts with what is the share of GDP. You pay a premium by being rich, so rich countries pay more per share of GDP than poor countries. And then we pay an additional premium by virtue of being a permanent member. So it was going down as our global share of GDP went down, and it has gone back up a little bit. So it is just a worth remembering the irony.

But I do not disagree with anything that Ambassador Negroponte said in terms of the need to keep pushing on this.

And it is an issue that is going to have to be made an important priority with the incoming Secretary General. They are going to have to make it clear to the incoming Secretary General that to sustain support for the United Nations, it is impossible to explain to the American public why we pay an outsized share of this bill.

It is true that we have an outsized interest—an outsized interest—in the performance. We are the only power that has interests in every region of the world and at the global level. So we have an outsized interest here as well.

And to a certain extent, in all honesty, that reduces our leverage. Everybody knows that we have an outsized interest in these things.

Senator CARDIN. Because we have assumed greater burdens, we have even greater burdens.

Dr. JONES. Correct.

Senator CARDIN. That is an interesting way of looking at it.

Let me ask one last question, if I might.

Ambassador Power was pretty firm and optimistic about the September 28 meeting of the countries that are contributing resources to the U.N. peacekeeping. The commitments, she continues to state, are just that—commitments. They have not been delivered yet.

Have you had a chance to review the September 28 results? And are you optimistic that, in fact, this will have greater participation by the countries that are capable of doing more? What is your prognosis on this?

Dr. JONES. Well, I had the honor of being invited to that meeting by the administration, so I was there for that. And I have been involved in helping the U.N. and the administration think through the preparation for it. I am semi-optimistic.

I think that the Europeans, in particular, as they have drawn down in Afghanistan, they have capabilities that they are not using. In that context, they can contribute. The Dutch in Mali I think are the most important example of what we have seen so far.

I think they recognize they have a deep interest that if they are going to come to terms with their migration problem and their refugee problem, they have to go and solve it in the places where it originates. So they have an interest in helping to stabilize conflicts in Africa and beyond. So I am somewhat optimistic.

I would be very optimistic were it not for a very different reality, which is Russia and Ukraine, which is causing European governments, fully understandably, to reprioritize back to some older kinds of concerns about NATO, about the containment of Russia, et cetera. That is going to put pressure on European defense budgets, and it is going to put pressure on European militaries to be worried about things other than conflicts in Africa.

And so the two things are, unfortunately, happening at the same time. I think there is a genuine will from Europeans and from the other countries like Korea that I mentioned to participate in U.N. peacekeeping. But at the same time, we are facing new challenges from China, from Russia, et cetera. Those are going to put different kinds of pressures.

So I think she is very right to push the argument. I think the administration is right to pursue that initiative. But there are going to be other challenges we confront at the same time that will I think diminish the full impact that it might have had otherwise, unfortunately.

Ambassador NEGROPONTE. I think we need to keep the spotlight on it. I think that was a great initiative by the President and has to be followed up.

The other thing I might add with respect to contributing countries is one encouraging region of the world in that regard is the willingness of certain Latin American countries to contribute to peacekeeping, global peacekeeping, which they have been reluctant to do in the past. I mean, the mention of Colombia, for example, and Brazil, too.

I thought that was encouraging, and I think it is something the U.N. needs to avail itself of.

Senator CARDIN. Thank you. Thank you both for your service.

The CHAIRMAN. Thank you.

One of the great privileges that we have around here is the access to people like you who are so respected and have the ability to share wisdom with us and experiences. We know that every day when we come to work, so we want to thank you for your continued involvement in issues of importance to our country. Thank you for being here today.

As you will see, a lot of our members make themselves present by asking questions later. So without objection, first of all, the record will be open until the close of business Friday. But if you could respond in a fairly timely manner, that would also be appreciated.

The CHAIRMAN. We thank you for your service to our country, and we thank you for being here today.

And with that, the meeting is adjourned.

[Whereupon, at 12:04 p.m., the hearing was adjourned.]

ADDITIONAL MATERIAL SUBMITTED FOR THE RECORD

RESPONSES TO QUESTIONS FOR THE RECORD SUBMITTED TO AMBASSADOR SAMANTHA POWER BY SENATOR BOB CORKER

Question. During the September U.N. Peacekeeping Summit, the United States, as well as other member states, made significant commitments to enhancing peacekeeping capabilities. The administration has stated that funding for this will not come from U.S. assessed contributions to international peacekeeping (CIPA account) but from elsewhere.

- What is the approximate funding figure the President will be requesting in his budget to fund these commitments?
- From what agencies and accounts will this funding be drawn?

Answer. The Leaders' Summit on September 28 generated commitments by 49 countries plus the EU, NATO, and African Union to contribute aviation, infantry, police, and other critical support to U.N. peacekeeping operations. The Summit demonstrated the multiplier effect that can occur when countries come together to address some of the world's most pressing problems.

The Department of State is participating in an interagency discussion about steps the United States can take to continue to ensure that the United Nations has the means to fulfill its role in preventing the outbreak, escalation, and spread of conflicts. The Department of Defense is an important partner in this discussion.

Currently we do not foresee new activities having any significant impact on FY 2016 funding requirements. There may be minor changes as we refocus some of our efforts, and we look forward to working with you on any adjustments going forward.

We are currently formulating the FY 2017 President's Budget, which will be presented to Congress in early February 2017, and we will consult with you regarding any resource requirements for FY 2017 at that time.

Question. I recently wrote to Secretary Kerry regarding steps to reduce the risk of peacekeeper sexual exploitation and abuse. This appears to be a chronic problem for the U.N. I understand that the U.S. Mission to the United Nations created an internal task force to address this issue and that an action plan exists.

- What policy proposals are being considered as part of the action plan and what steps will you take to implement them?
- Do you think this is a priority for the current U.N. leadership? If so, what makes you believe that this time is different?
- How will the U.S. Mission at the United Nations press the next Secretary General to maintain the momentum on addressing sexual exploitation and abuse?

Answer. The U.S. Mission to the U.N. created an internal task force on sexual exploitation and abuse (SEA) to take a serious look at the causes of and solutions to SEA in U.N. peacekeeping, a reflection of our government-wide commitment to preventing SEA. The measures the task force is reviewing include how best to support and/or put pressure on the U.N. and its member states as appropriate. The task force is examining how best to engage member states, both bilaterally and through multilateral fora, on both better policy and practice.

The U.N. Secretary-General has expressed deep commitment to the initiatives he championed regarding SEA, as seen outlined in his latest reports involving SEA, including his own implementation report on the recommendations of the High Level Independent Panel on Peace Operations. Next, we expect that his February 2016 annual report on SEA will provide country-specific information on those troop and police contributing countries (TCCs/PCCs) whose uniformed personnel face credible allegations of SEA.

More broadly, the U.N. is in the process of implementing more than 40 proposals from the Secretary-General's February 2015 report. The most significant measures include: establishing immediate response teams in peacekeeping missions to gather and preserve evidence for use in investigations; adopting a six-month timeline for completion of investigations of SEA and calling on member states to adhere to the same timeline; strengthening its complaint reception framework to ensure mechanisms are in place within communities where people can come forward, in confidence, to raise complaints regarding U.N. personnel; strengthening administrative measures against civilian staff members found to have committed SEA, including withholding entitlements; suspending pay to TCCs/PCCs for personnel accused of SEA on the basis of credible allegations; and, setting out the framework for a trust fund to provide support and assistance to survivors and children born as a result of sexual exploitation and abuse by U.N. peacekeepers.

We will begin discussions on the issue of sexual misconduct with the next Secretary-General from the beginning of his or her tenure, to ensure that reforms set in motion by the current Secretary-General are strengthened and institutionalized, and to urge the next Secretary-General's continued engagement. We will continue to press at all levels, in New York, in the field, and with troop and police contributing countries on this serious issue.

Question. With respect to peacekeeping operations, generally speaking, the U.N. Security Council authorizes the mission while the U.N. Secretary General, through the office of peacekeeping operations, runs the mission.

- How actively involved is the U.N. Security Council in oversight of the mission? How often does the Council travel to review a mission's operations and progress, firsthand?
- What are your thoughts on having the U.N. Security Council establish, for each mission, its own ombudsman with full authority to review and conduct oversight of the peacekeeping mission and who would report directly to the Security Council when mission mandates are renewed?

Answer. As the body responsible for authorizing U.N. peacekeeping operations, the Security Council (UNSC) actively seeks and receives through several different channels reporting, briefings, and other information to oversee each mission's performance. Such information is critically important in helping the UNSC to determine what each mission's mandate should be, the size and composition of the force needed, the duration of the mandate, as well as any other needed changes or adjustments.

The UNSC makes trips, as needed and as possible, throughout the year to peacekeeping missions and trouble spots. For example, during 2015, Security Council members visited Haiti, the Central African Republic, and Burundi, as well as the headquarters of the African Union in Addis Ababa. However, the UNSC's primary oversight is conducted in New York. The formal channels for UNSC oversight include written reports by the Secretary-General to the UNSC, which the Council generally requests on a quarterly or semi-annual basis; regular oral briefings to the UNSC by U.N. officials, as well as by the Special Representative of the Secretary-General (SRSG) responsible for a particular peacekeeping mission; and consultations in the UNSC on mandate renewal resolutions in which UNSC members discuss any changes needed to a mission's mandate. Such changes may include updates to the mandated tasks, associated increases or reductions in the number of uniformed personnel, and modifications in the composition of the force. The Council can also request additional assessments of missions when it is considering reconfiguration, drawdown, or transition. The Council often asks the Secretary-General to identify benchmarks for progress and to incorporate an evaluation of the mission against those benchmarks in his regular reports.

Council members also have access to a number of other oversight materials produced by various U.N. mechanisms, such as the U.N.'s Office of Internal Oversight Services (OIOS), which provides oversight for the larger U.N. system; its audits and evaluation reports are available online. The Secretary-General also releases annual budget performance reports on each peacekeeping operation.

The United States continues to press the U.N. for greater oversight of its peace-keeping missions, particularly in the areas of financial controls and conduct and discipline. We believe the conduct and discipline units in missions must be stronger and better staffed. The United States was instrumental in the creation of, and supports the strengthening of, the Office of the Director for Peacekeeping Strategic Partnership, which is intended to provide services akin to an inspector general to identify gaps that affect the delivery of mandates by U.N. peacekeeping missions and make recommendations on systemic issues related to U.N. peacekeeping operations. We also believe that more comprehensive reporting by the Secretary-General on performance would improve the Council's ability to exercise its oversight responsibilities. We have called for and support the U.N.'s evaluation of the impact of specific mandated tasks, such as the U.N.'s current revamping of its indicators to evaluate the impact of protection of civilians tasks.

The idea of the UNSC directly appointing an ombudsperson for each U.N. peacekeeping mission raises a number of issues that require careful consideration, including:

- Scope of Mandate: The Council would need to determine the issues appropriately addressed by an ombudsperson to avoid conflicting with the oversight responsibilities of the SRSG for the management of his/her mission's personnel and resources or the existing auditing, conduct and discipline, performance, and evaluation mechanisms in the U.N. system, including those mentioned above.
- *Relationship vis-a-vis the SRSG:* Currently, the SRSG is responsible for overseeing the overall effectiveness of the mission under his or her charge. The appointment of an ombudsperson raises the potential for conflicting signals between SRSGs and Force Commanders and ombudspersons, which could be counterproductive to the mission's performance if such dynamics undermine the authority of the SRSG or the Force Commander to direct and manage the mission or their strategies for achieving the mission's mandate.
- *Selection Process and Funding Issues:* The Council would need to determine how it would select ombudspersons and their staffs, if not through the Secretary-General. It would also have to determine how to fund ombudspersons positions and staffs if the positions were not established through the UNGA Fifth Committee process. We would welcome further staff-level discussions on this idea.

Question. Unfortunately, peacekeepers sometimes commit acts of violence against the people they have been sent to protect. The Convention on Privileges and Immunities of the United Nations (Article VIII, Section 29) states that the U.N. "shall make provisions for appropriate modes of settlement" with respect to disputes. This would include claims by civilians hurt by the negligence or intentional acts of U.N. personnel or those under their authority.

- It is my understanding that since 1990, the United Nations has not once created a standing claims commission despite 32 Status of Forces Agreements providing for the creation of one in the event of damages. If true, why has the U.N. not taken steps to address this problem?
- With respect to establishing such modes of settlement or claims commissions, do you support the principle that the TCCs responsible for misconduct should pay any damages for harm caused by the officers and soldiers who serve under its flag?

Answer. It is also our understanding that the U.N. has generally settled claims through local claims review boards, and that neither the U.N. nor the host countries have created standing claims commissions referenced in status of forces agreements (SOFAs) between the U.N. and host countries. A local claims review board is an internal board established within a U.N. Mission, responsible for settling third party claims in country. A local claims review board can also refer a claim to U.N. Headquarters for approval or disapproval if the settlement amount exceeds the authorized limit of the board. Local claims review boards have generally been effective in resolving instances of negligence.

We support the idea that the U.N. should provide appropriate victims' assistance related to misconduct by U.N. peacekeepers, and understand that the U.N. is currently working on a policy to devise such a system of assistance in the context of sexual exploitation and abuse (SEA) cases.

Abuses and violations committed by peacekeepers are unacceptable, undermine a peacekeeping mission's ability to carry out its mandate, and damage a mission's relationship with the community.

Question. Does the U.N. system have in place protocols to disbar contractors who have been found by a competent authority to be guilty of negligence or intentional acts which have led to injuries or deaths among a host country population? If not, should the U.N. establish such a system of debarment?

Answer. Chapter 7 of the United Nations Procurement Manual provides for suspension or removal from the U.N.'s Register of Vendors of any vendor under formal investigation or sanctioned by a national authority for engaging in proscribed practices that include, but are not limited to, corruption, fraud, coercion, collusion, obstruction, and other unethical practices.

Chapter 7 of the Procurement Manual also provides for suspension or removal of a vendor for actions that create financial, operational, reputational and other undue risks to the United Nations. Negligent or intentional acts that were harmful to a host country population would fall within the realm of proscribed activities for which a contractor would be removed the U.N.'s list of eligible vendors.

○